Compelling Allure

Compelling Allure

"Compelling Allure"

By

Princess Hester

"FINDING, ATTRACTING AND EMBRACING THE BEAUTY IN LIFE EVEN WHEN TIMES GET TOUGH."

ISBN: 9781701663237

A Memoir about the traumatic life events, the battle of depression and anxiety that built my endurance and the battles I fought to create a life of peace, harmony and understanding of life's ultimate purpose.

Compelling Allure

"COMPELLING ALLURE"

Table of Contents

Introduction

FIND YOUR INNER PEACE!

Where ever you are, whatever challenging situation you're dealing with, there is harmony in the end. I've realized that life will bring us to places where we never expected to be. We don't have a crystal ball. I've always believed in being prepared for the unexpected. When I prepared for something, for some reason; I never felt prepared! It is hard to be prepared for something that isn't placed right in front of us. It's like I've constantly put myself in positions by habit. When you are used to a particular way of life, it becomes a safe haven.

It is a place that feels secure and also the norm. However that can become dangerous depending on the habit that you have; drugs, sex, abuse, hurt, trauma, etc. These are all negative habits to get used to. You have to find out a way to get unused of the old you.

I believe that fear keeps people from moving forward in life. It's hard to adjust to a positive way of life. Also some people feel forced and don't have another way out. Well if this is you; understand that everyone experiences a level of some kind of habit, temptation, obstacles and fear. It's normal! I am here to tell you that there are ways to work through it.

"Don't allow your current circumstances to become your reality."

In

2015, I began to go through a "*quarter mid-life crisis.*" I call it that because I'm not old enough to have had an actual "*mid-life crisis.*" However, I have experienced a lot with in a short time frame and I've yet to reach my thirties. I was recently enrolled in college pursuing my bachelor's degree. It was a sunny afternoon and I was overwhelmed with homework.

My son who was three years old at the time wanted to play outside with the other kids who were in the yard. I watched him from the door as he played. Then suddenly I went into shock (everything around me stopped as I seen Noah run towards the ball that only had touched the sidewalk. That was enough to make me nervous. I saw visions of a car flying down the street and I ran towards him yelling,

"No!"

Soon after, I went into the house because I felt light headed. It was an unimaginable feeling; a feeling of confusion, misconceptions as well as fear. At that moment I felt my life flashed before my eyes, when suddenly I had a panic attack. It felt like my last breath was being taken. My life felt like death; not knowing that it would have changed my life forever.

Through this challenging time in my life, I found myself isolated, filled with many thoughts; which later led me to anxiety. I knew that there was so much going on in my life that hit me all at once. I was a single mother with two kids, a part time job with little income, full time student and daily life. During this process I was not living a healthy lifestyle. My social life consisted of individuals who weren't in the best interest for me. I began to drink socially. Then I began to drink more often which resulted in loss of friendships, relationships and almost my life on multiple occasions.

I needed a breakthrough on a spiritual level. I decided that I had to seek therapy because I knew that I could not do it on my own. At this point I had gained weight. I had low self-esteem. I was experiencing anxiety attacks every other day. I had attacks while driving to work, road trips, at home, and church. I was hopeless and ultimately felt that I had no reason to live.

It was a heavy weight on my shoulders that I couldn't shake. I was not anywhere prepared for the unexpected. If I had prepared myself mentally, maybe I could've avoided a lot of hurt and pain that I brought into my life.

We can't do it alone. We all need somebody even the ones who feel strong, because you are stronger when you take the chance to admit you are in need. It doesn't make you weak.

Depending on one's philosophy, there could be multiple interpretations on what a crisis is. My theology is that we live in a society where we are exposed to so many things that have an effect on how we view life. The over consumption forces us to absorb everything including the superficial. We tend to get accustomed to a particular way of life based on events that we've experienced or have seen others experience. It took me quite some time to break habits that were embedded in me.

Remember the seasons are constantly changing. Sometimes we don't know what season we are in because of what we see. What we see is not the full reality of the truth. It is the hidden figures and the unseen things that are the truth. When the winter arrives we do not see the beautiful flowers. It is not until the season begins to change. However, through the winter the plant is preparing itself. It doesn't look compelling at all. It is the same with us.

We often times look in the mirror at ourselves only to self-criticize. If we took the time to realize that there are things that are working in us, everything else will come together. When the seasons change, the flowers begin to break through the surface. At this time it is being nourished being underneath. Over time we begin to come into our own. What you see is not the finished product. God is working on some things so you have to keep pushing through because there is a season called *"Harvest Season!"* It is when the things that have been unseen begin to manifest and the beauty that was living within in comes alive.

"This is the season of reason. Keep nourishing your dreams and hopes. What is your aspiration? Let that lead you, because you have to have a goal with a purpose. Without a purpose you are working towards something that you'll never be able to truly identify the essence of."

I always tried to figure out what the purpose of life was. I was overwhelmed and became confused with the concept. I

disconnected from who I was as an individual. I

lost myself because I was unclear about what I

was doing in my life. I wasn't living on purpose.

I was living hesitantly because I didn't know

what God had kept for me. You have to live on

purpose because if not your alive on the

outside, but in the inside you could feel the

total opposite.

When I was younger, I wanted to be

happy and for things to go *"right"*. I didn't know

that I was in search of something much

greater, until I began to reconnect with myself.

I began to love myself and began being

intentional. We become uncomfortable

because when we aren't doing the things that

matter, we become stagnant. I wasn't aware

that it was going to be a battle. We then

develop a way of life that depends on particular

satisfactions. We ignore the

feelings inside that prevent

us from tackling what truly hurts us. We look

for distractions; whether it's an activity, hanging

with friends or materialistic things. We should

be taking action and not allowing fear to block

us from our reality.

In order to reconnect with yourself, you

have to be grounded. When you are in the

midst of everything, it feels like there's no way

out. I'm here to tell you that there is. Keep the

faith and work towards a goal each and every

day. I ensure you something magical will come

out of it. If not keep trying until it manifest. Are

you willing to make sacrifices and have an

understanding that happiness is within? It is

not given to you; it is priceless. I'm sorry to tell

you, but you cannot buy happiness. Happiness is a learned behavior- our upbringing, what we see, the decisions that we make in life.

In order to be happy and for it to be sustainable, you must explore different ways to fulfill joyous moments that are everlasting. We don't buy the things because we want it for temporary pleasure. In the midst of buying things we have the idea that it is what is needed to give us happiness and we try to avoid the fact that it is not going to give us everlasting inner peace. It will give you peace for that moment, but once it expires then your happiness goes with it.

We buy the things that we don't need because we feel that we should already have those things or simply because we want to have the *"finer things in life"*. Why is it that we feel entitled to it! It's almost like we're waiting for a rescue or waiting for the right time to be happy. Instead of embracing what is right in front of us. We get sucked into life through temptations and the flesh. The media deems unrealistic lifestyles into society which creates a platform and we do the things that we feel are acceptable in society; opposed to doing the things that we feel will make a difference in our life as well as others.

You have to learn how to be the center of your own attention by focusing on the betterment of yourself. Some people may call it selfish, but I call it self-love. Personally I felt that I should have been more fortunate. I blamed my childhood and my upbringing as to why I am not as successful as I should have been. "Struggle" was not in my agenda.

Looking back I wish I knew that what we wanted was temporary versus the things that we needed would lead us to eternity. I want a long lasting pleasure.

It is so easy to get caught up with temporary pleasures only to feel disappointed in the end. You end up finding out that the things that you wanted wasn't necessarily what you needed. I want the pleasure of waking up knowing that even if my life isn't as ideal, that each and every day I have the opportunity to make a change in my life by being intentional. What kind of life do you want? Do you want a life that is based on temporary pleasures?

We live in a society where education is everything so we feed ourselves all the information that we need to get to the next level. However, what we do with the information truly makes a difference. The information that we apply to our lives determines our outcome. "*Fill your mind with healthy things, prepare your mind and try to work on it by exercising positive thoughts.*" I've read leadership and improvement books; I've also listened to motivational speakers. I've looked at astrology articles.

Why do we feel the need to educate our self so much, but don't apply all the information. If we are not applying with our actions then how are we making a difference? We practice repetitive behaviors, habits and depend on validation from others, when we should rely on our soul and faith.

Based on our upbringing shapes how we see things in life as an individual. We use our childhood experiences and become stagnant not allowing our ideas to flow. I always felt good knowing that someone cared about be. It made me feel noticed and appreciated. I always found myself trying to connect with people who felt that I was important. The reason that I developed this habit is because of the feeling of instant gratification. I realized that over time I was becoming selfish and disappointed.

It is important to know your value and your self -worth. Are you profitable or are you depleted? I had to become selfless. If you can't value yourself, it will be hard for others to value you. You have to find the true person that you are deep inside. It's not an easy task, but if you seek you will find. Look at yourself from within.

Who are you? Who are your trying to be? What is it that you want out of life? Learning

how to differentiate who I was from my desire
of who I thought I should have been or could
have been, it tore me apart. I was afraid to face
my self and become selfless because I had a
difficult time trying to accept things as they
were.

In society the media deems this ideal
Image and lifestyle that we think is the way of
life. It is so confusing, and when I would look
at myself in the mirror; I'd see this beautiful,
intelligent, innocent and naive young woman.
She would then compare herself to every
woman on Instagram and Facebook only to be
left with a lot of disappointments! When I
realized that I was a unique individual, my life
began to shift. I became frustrated when I
see the things that matter in society. I couldn't
understand why I was alone with the

perception that I had.

What happened to humanity? I think what hurts us the most is denial and then comes fear. If we could just admit to the things that we don't enjoy doing, people's lives would feel lighter and clearer. The more we live in denial, our denial baggage becomes heavier and overwhelming. When we face these fears, we feel invincible. The truth will set you free no matter how long it takes you.

"No Pain leaves you anywhere. You must fight the battle or you won't gain. The more that you are true to yourself, the more you become aware of the societal and environmental impact nature has on us subconsciously."

I found myself getting lost in life. I thought I had to look a particular way, talk and act. Many people become stuck in this ongoing battle of finding their identity. I found it very hard to connect with who I was. You don't realize that the things on the earth hinders us because it's all an illusion. With all the outside distractions, it can often times disconnect you from your truth. My favorite quote is: *"We are in this world, We are not of this world."*

We naturally want control. We may not want to admit it, but it is true. We want to control how much money that we make, our career, materialistic things, pleasures etc. Inevitably things end up happening and we lose sense of control. What do you do then? How do you react? Until we have an understanding that there are some things that we cannot control even if we tried over and over. Sometimes it becomes a job because we are constantly working towards having *"full control".*

I believe that we have control to a certain extent; to the extent of the decisions that we make and how we handle life when it becomes tough or unbearable. It is important to be self-aware; we have to be willing to shift our ways. We never know when that time will be over. So yes it is essential that we live in the now. Living in the now doesn't mean, *"Living your life like it's your last"* and making irrational decisions. If we do not do it now, we don't know when you'll have the next opportunity?

We have this thing call time. It wouldn't matter if there were forty-eight hours in a day, would you actually be satisfied. It's a delusion. You're constantly changing; so it's a must that we find ways to adapt ourselves rather than losing the person we are destined to be.

Adaptation is the one of the hardest transitions. What was presented to me at an early age dictated my perceptions and conceptions of life. We start to adapt to our environment because naturally we have biological traits that are inherited.

We have the ability to adapt to most environments, but sometimes we end up in places that may appear foreign or unfamiliar. It's a requirement. It is okay to feel uncomfortable sometimes, as long as it is because you are working towards something that could contribute to positive change in your life. These are the experiences that shape you into the person that God has intended for you to be.

Adaptation is not for everyone; it is not easy and everyone has his or her own pace.

Finding ways to adapt in a changing world is often difficult. It is scary to do something different when it has been working for you or even feel more comfortable. For me, I was forced to adapt due to the life decisions that I made. I decided to have children at a young age due to not having protected sex. I failed inevitably, purposely due to fear. I wanted the best for myself so I had to take chances.

"What got us to those circumstances? What did we do and what didn't we do to get us there?"

I honestly didn't have a clue of what was promised for me. I ultimately just wanted control. We often make excuses as to why we are where we are, but only to realize for me, that we create the world around us- you control your destiny. You have the opportunity to choose where you want to go and what you want to achieve, however you may not be able to control them to its entirety due to the unexpected. If you feel that you don't, you may need to make some transitions in your life.

Based on the choices that we make, it can be a barrier and block you from making progress. Your current circumstance doesn't dictate your truth and what you are working towards. Sometimes we look at what is in front of us such as circumstances, but we don't look underneath the surface.

It is what makes us unique. If we deny where we come from, if we deny what's beneath the surface, then how can we approve the outcome?

The shocking sudden moments that take place in our lives are the ones that stop us from moving forward. The key is to not let your thoughts dictate who you are and make your life a lie. Seeing what is in front of us is superficial. We don't allow ourselves to look at the beneath surface, clean it up and work our way back up. We often get stuck in the same position.

I believe that there are situations that are presented to us that will be represented until we are able to make a different decision. We want instant gratification so we look at what is right in front of us, feeling lost and confused as to why it is the way it is .We can re-program ourselves by practicing positive thinking habits.

This will develop your mind in many ways and you'll be able to take advantage. When you practice being positive you not only become positive, but you start to attract the same kind of people. It's not an easy task because the world and its over consumption can become our life greatest burden. If we work at the surface, we then manifest a life filled with abundance, rather than a superficial life that is filled with hurt, pain and corruption that lies beneath the surface. Life is about working through obstacles and being true to "yourself". "We cannot hide or cover the things that we have faced.

It is common for people to have a lot on their plate. Not because we are forced to, but because of the inevitable. One thing we can't change is the life that was given to us because it already has been written. Spiritually speaking, I do believe that our life is predestined. We can go through hoops just to get to a place that God wants us to be. Don't allow that to hinder your life journey, because you can always have the ability to create a new way of thinking and take action, but don't take the shortcut. It is better to finish last rather than first, because sometimes you need to come faced with experiences that you can learn from in the long run.

"We are all on a journey with different maps."

Only time can tell us where we should be. Our destiny dictates how we will get there. Our thoughts create our reality. What you do with your time is crucial! We all face many obstacles and shouldn't allow others' opinions validate who we are. Our minds are interchangeable as well as our physical appearance to a certain extent.

According to the National Science Foundation in 2005, it stated that the research on human thoughts estimated that we have 12,000 to 60,000 thoughts per day, the common human being has fifty to seventy thousand thoughts a day on average, that is 2,500 thoughts per hour in 24 hours.

Therefore we have to train our minds to have as many positive thoughts to overrule the negative ones. It's like a war in our mind. We have to learn and practice how to fight off the enemies without getting killed. The more we fight, fail and let them take control, the fewer chances that we have to win the battle. The negative thoughts will know that your positive thoughts can be

"The mind plays a major part in how far that power will go. If you allow your mind to take in so much without any boundaries or outlets, you become a bomb ready to explode."

34

destroyed because the amount of times you allowed them to win.

The clearer the picture becomes, the more you can be at ease with your mind in tune into reality. You have to surrender and let your strength lead you to your dream. If you don't feel that you have the strength, then seek and you shall find. If you suffer from any mental health problems this could be an experience that has many obstacles. Remember to keep fighting!

We have to let go of our egos to see how strong we actually are. You are powerful in your own way, but you should try and be mindful of the impact that it could have on your life. Power can be weakness. People tend to have this idea that if you have power, they are invincible. Then you're looked at as important or superior to others. Power comes in many different sizes, shapes and forms. You can be the top executive at a reputable company, making six figures and living the dream. Well that's the basic ideology of power is, *"someone who is in control."* They are superior to most.

If you suffer from any anxiety, this is a way to test your abilities as an individual. You hear about famous people who started from nothing and became wealthy. In reality you have to take a step back and think where they came from. How they might have been impacted mentally, emotionally and physically. You hear the same things about motivational speakers, preachers, life coaches, etc. It isn't easy trying to separate the mind from the reality. The key is to have a strong and determined mind that can take in the good and bad, and know how to utilize both in a positive way.

It's ok to have negative encounters in life. It exposes you to the real world. It is all a test to determine how you are able to handle situations and learn from them. It is also a way to determine your strength. As you work on your self to build your mind by creating healthy habits, you will start to realize that without certain encounters that you have experienced; you might have been lost at the time. It is time to find what you have lost along the way!

What I mean by this is that we all face obstacles in life. Some of the obstacles are a lot heavier than others. In the process we lose hope and you have to gain that back because it is essential to the betterment of you! If I had allowed the obstacles I faced to take over my life, I would not have been able to tell my story to you as you are reading this. Even though the obstacles that I faced in my life may have seemed negative, they helped me tremendously.

Embrace your journey and motivate others.

I made it my duty to find the good within every obstacle that I have faced. Due to my experiences, I learned that the obstacles made me stronger and gave me power. I never felt successful. I know you are wondering how. No matter what others may think or feel about you it doesn't matter in the end.

"A lot of times we view ourselves in ways where we are hard on ourselves. As I am growing, I realized that everything isn't a flaw. Being different is what makes us unique."

It matters when you don't know who you are or where you are going. I always felt like a failure because I had a philosophy that I had to meet criteria. I always changed my look.

My appearance overall was based on wanting to be accepted. Over time I had reoccurring thoughts that later on in life led to anxiety.

Why be anxious? I realized one day that I couldn't live like that anymore and decided to eliminate some of the clutter that was exceeding the space I had in my mind. I felt like an atomic bomb ready to explode. The over consumption that I had inside was taking over my life, literally. I became sick and didn't have a purpose; I was only living through the grace of God.

When you allow failure to take over

your life, you then feel that you are trapped. I was feeding my mind with negativity. I had reoccurring thoughts of death, my funeral date and never being successful. It is essential to embrace the person that you are and to realize that we cannot *"control"* everything.

Remember there are some things that we can control to an extent. What we can control is the way that we perceive things in life. This message will lead you through my hard journey to a strong, powerful and disciplined mind that will leave you feeling fearless, strengthened, motivated, important, compassionate and ready to face life for what it is. Not for what you think it should be.

Darkness

"Be Fearless and Find What You Are Afraid Of"

In this lifetime you will encounter many obstacles. Have you ever woke up feeling lost, wondering what your next move was going to be or laid down for hours in a state of confusion, worries and pain? I believe that in order to become greater, the greatest has encountered very low points in his or her life. We wake up with the intentions of having a great day filled with happiness, but oftentimes when you're suffering from depression, anxiety, or similar mental health complications, your mind reroutes your perspective and outlook on the reality. Your thoughts then become you- because you're constantly living in your mind. There is nothing worse than waking up and your mind's racing with thoughts, or if you are in the community and you have anxiety unexpectantly.

This happened to me often, even when I thought that going on vacation would change things. I would still have anxiety attacks. Some of the reasons are because I wasn't taking care of myself, I was being stubborn and was also afraid. You want to address the problem early on because it is harder to reverse once you are deep in the *"mind battle"*. One summer day my mother and I decided to go to Atlantic City. Suddenly on the way there, I asked to stop to get water because I couldn't swallow. I was frustrated and would be anxious for no reason. My mother was nervous and I could feel her energy. She was afraid for my life and didn't know how to address my problem because she couldn't even if she tried. *"The pain was a feeling that made me want to die."*

Although I was living, I couldn't enjoy the great things in life as simple as going on a road trip. I remember telling my mother that I wouldn't wish that experience on anyone's life and that I would trade anxiety for anything else. On the way back home from the trip, I had a full-blown anxiety attack. My mother had to call 911 to meet us off of the exit because she didn't know what the outcome would be. I was taken to the hospital by the ambulance and had to stay there until my pressure was regular. I knew at this moment that I had to figure out a way to get out of the darkness.

Whatever thoughts you have whether they are negative or positive; it dictates how you will maneuver on a daily basis. Your thoughts can lead you to anxiety and depression.

It is important to cater to it as soon as possible. Don't become your own enemy like I did. Life doesn't have a map or guide that we can use to lead us to our intended destination, only our actions does. My experiences led me to fighting for my life because I wanted to live in despite of feeling hurt inside. We don't have the ability to know where we need to go or where we need to stop. This can lead you to feeling uncomfortable. All you can do is take a chance, by choosing to make decisions you feel is the best for you. Focus on the possibilities and the rest will come.

The question is what if you're unaware of what is best for you? I remember growing up and people would tell me what they thought was best for me. I find that it is easy to get caught up in wanting other people approval. I really got tired of hearing what people thought I should be doing, how I should dress, what I should be interested in and etc.

This problem could become very contradicting and cause many issues in someone's life. Even the way that I dressed and did my hair just like no one could ever accept me for me. I really felt like this little girl who was just the "ugliest girl" in the world. No matter what I did, no matter how many times I change my hair, or how many times I change my style of clothing. On the other hand there were also people who told me that I would

never amount to the things that I thought I

would. I could never fit in and I just didn't

understand. You have to be willing to find the

beauty within yourself, because it is the only

way to

escape.

"Embrace Who you are. Stop looking at the person that people want you to be."

Over time I became insecure because

what I thought was best for me was overlooked

majority of the time. When you are doing the

things that truly make you happy, your world

begins to change. You want to live a life that

you know will leave you feeling weightless.

Often times, people end up living for someone

else rather than living for what they truly

believe in. The problem that I think makes life more difficult to accept is when an individual is aware that they are living for someone else. After living a lie for so long I became defensive and wanted to do everything independently. I had come to a realization that I was missing out in my life.

I didn't think I had the tools to even understand what was best for me at the time. I only had an idea. I have lived most of my life in fear afraid to make choices for myself because I allowed people to make choices for me.

When I did make choices for myself, I almost always seem to fail. I felt like I couldn't get anything right because everything that I did, I got criticized.-Every thought that I ever had went unnoticed and to top it off I had no father figure in my life. The only light I had in this darkness was the light from the faith that I've always carried and the light from my mother. Although I was young I've always wanted to seek more in life. I knew that I had another Father, which was the one above. What most people run into is that dead end. Well where do I go next? How do I get there? Well what if I get lost? I have lived my whole life wanting control and it didn't get me anywhere.

"You are better off taking a chance in life rather than staying in one place. If you stay in one place, you'll never have the opportunity to get lost."

I realized that life itself cannot be controlled. But we can in fact control our destiny. How can I control something that I'm just a part of? This built up a lot of anxiety over time. We can have control and it's your mind that allows you the opportunity. When you spend your life trying to not get lost you end up getting lost anyway.

The more obstacles that you face in life, the more likely you are able to get over life's greatest burdens. However, some people live a perfect life not making any mistakes not getting lost; perfect family, perfect job and the white picket fence. I on the other hand decided to get into anything that I could get myself into. I was in the terrible two stages for two decades of my life.

The unexpected happened in my life when I was in my early teens; I had come in contact with a man who became my father instantly. It changed my life for the better. As I got older this man gave me a lot of wisdom that I can appreciate. My dad always told me that, *"A hard head would make a soft ass."* You can trick your mind into whatever you think life is. You can do it for the better to develop positive ways of thinking or you can tell your self-negative things. The key is to not continue to make the same mistakes. For some, you may be in control of life. For others it may seem it's beyond it.

My whole life I've suffered mentally. At a young age I realized that my mind was a lot more complex than my appropriate age group. My mind was continuously going. It was like a train on a track that couldn't stop; my mind wouldn't rest. I would think of everything that no one probably could ever think of. I was able to solve solutions of certain situations quicker than others. I was always insightful and asked

many questions. I wanted to know everything

there was in life and I tried to experience it all.

"When you are seeking for inner peace,
you will find yourself in situations that
you never thought you would be."

I've always had a deeper insight with the

way that I perceived everything that was in and

outside of my life. Internally I

couldn't understand my thoughts. Throughout

my childhood I always looked for validation

from my mom without a doubt. She never had

any answers for me. She then blamed herself

for my misery. She thought it was the lack of

support due to the fact we had no family

around us because we lived in Connecticut and

the rest of our family lived in North Carolina. She blamed society and carried guilt.

I was a child but I didn't understand the effect I had on my family. I was very hard on myself and I depended on other's validation to identify myself. I was a kid who just didn't understand myself. It was scary because I did not know why I had so many questions between my younger years of age until my adult years. It was frustrating and made me a lot different than my friends. I was way more mature at an earlier age.

I wanted things like a family and other validations to make me feel whole because I could not understand what it

"We don't realize that we are born into pain and sometimes it is by default; luckily you can change your reality."

was that I was missing. I felt an empty space in

my heart like a deep hole in my soul.

I was born into her world and endured her pain. It's almost like I was experiencing the pain that I was going to encounter throughout my lifetime. What I think happened looking back, I believe God was preparing me. The same cry that I had as a little girl is the same cry that I had as an adult. I cried and cried because I just wanted answers. When I was a child, I didn't have any gratitude. I had childish ways. I had pain and sorrow written all over my face. I wanted the wholeness of life. I wanted what was in store for my life at such a young age. I was very desperate.

At nine years of age that may have seemed to be impossible. I was aware that I wanted to be happier, but didn't have the tools to justify it. When you don't have the right resources and lack of knowledge it is hard to figure out what is necessary. I don't think that there was a possible way for me to understand what was happening in my life, let alone justify the feelings and emotions that I was experiencing; the mental battles, the thoughts of suicide and then the thoughts turned into depression.

How could a nine-year-old girl possibly be depressed? You live in a society where we automatically blame the parents, but what you don't realize is that mental health plays a major role. As a black woman, that is a topic or label that is looked at in a negative way. People would look at me and always told me how beautiful I was, but it never seemed to be enough. They admired how beautiful I was. My mother and her co-workers thought I was gorgeous. They even asked me to model for a Fashion Bug flyer, which is a clothing store. At that time I didn't have the tools to identify it. All I saw was a black girl with nappy hair who had to fight through it.

> *"The mind is powerful and so are you. Never give up on yourself but always strive for peace."*

Every day I woke up I compared myself to every other little girl. I just did not understand why every time I looked at myself I could not see the beauty that others seen. This darkness in my life felt like I was in a dark tunnel with no ending, no outlet to peace.

Internally you can feel pain, so when you look at yourself your mind is telling you that you are hurt. So you develop this way of thinking and it reflects how you look externally. In life it is hard to develop new ways of thinking when your mind is accustomed to the details you have programed your mind to act on internally and externally. I realized that through this time in my life I've always been determined and wanted to seek a full understanding on how the universe actually operated. We all want one thing and that's peace within ourselves. On one of Sarah Jakes' podcast, she said that there are young women who are trapped in that body that they used to be in and now they're an adult and afraid to let go of her. That was me!

I was a young girl who encountered so much pain. I had seen so much abuse including physical abuse and self-destruction. I had been a victim of rape at the age of 15. How could I embrace being a young woman and letting go of the fear of being that woman

56

when all I was used to was being that young abused girl. We sometimes need to seek understanding in order to live in harmony. I thought that happiness was something that was genetically implanted into us. The reality is that life comes with many barriers, lessons, teachings, and grey areas. Happiness is a choice and practice by behavior.

If you are suffering from any mental health complications such as depression and anxiety, it isn't easy to read something like this. My purpose of writing this book is to raise awareness for people who suffer from mental health. I suffered with mental health my whole life and I'll tell you it was a battle each and every day. I decided to continue to fight. I am here to make other people aware of mental health because it is not something that should be taken lightly and should go unnoticed because we all have some level of trauma, pain or anxiety. Also for individuals who feel that they may be at risk or their loved ones should be made aware. My life has been an ongoing rollercoaster and it hasn't been easy. I'm assuming you want to break this cycle.

> *"It is easier said than done because when you are the person dealing with pain, it feels like it will never end. But I am here to tell you that there are ways to cope and overcome."*

The key is, you have to want it bad and you can do it. It's almost like working out; you go at it for days, months or even years and it starts to become a part of your life. You don't see the results right away and this is where it could be a struggle. You have to fight through it. You have to want it so bad that it hurts to the core. It sometimes feels like your torturing yourself. Remember nothing in life that is worth having comes easy. Keep pushing and before you know it, it becomes you. The mind is tricky and if you're suffering at this moment look at yourself in the mirror and give yourself a big tight hug because this isn't an easy step.

"The longer that you wait to fight the battle, the harder the battle is to fight."

Fear is the biggest setback for a lot of us and to admit that you or your loved one is suffering isn't easy. Here's the problem, if you just sit back and allow life to happen without seeking help for yourself or someone else, life will get ahead of you. People are in this life, but not in reality and life can get behind you.

People oftentimes commit suicide because

that's the only escape. Don't let that be yours.

You or your loved one deserves a chance.

When you're suffering from any kind of hurt,

pain, oppression, and traumatic encounters, it

is easy to lose self. You may become irritable

and never feel satisfied. You may feel like what

you do is never enough. If you allow your mind

to control you, it will. If you let someone take

advantage of you, they will.

First step is recognizing the problem

you're facing. If your loved one is suffering, you

may not be doing enough according to them.

When you are broken, it is hard to see the

positives in anything and to think logically.

Everything appears black and white and

there's no light. When you see black and white,

you become used to it. You're a product of

your environment and you start to become

camouflage. Don't allow that to happen. Come

out of it. Now these are facts in this next

statement.

I can't swim to save my life. Due to this,

I had lived my whole life afraid of water being

over my head. When I was twelve years old, I

went to Las Vegas for a summer trip with my

aunt, uncle and brother. Unfortunately, I was

extremely excited and felt the need to jump in.

Take note seriously. When I jumped in, it was 4

ft. higher than what I anticipated. When I

jumped into the pool, the water immersed over

my head. I felt like I was non-existent and I was

afraid for my life.

No one was there and it felt like the end

of everything. That happened for about a half a

second literally. After I jumped up and latched my hands on to the edge of the pool because I did not want to drown. Drowning was never in me.

"Sometimes it takes something that serious to happen in your life for you to not want to make that same mistake."

Now I carried this fear and it had affected my whole life. I've been cautious with so many things that had literally blurred my ability to make logical decisions. So many things were going on in my then twelve year old body. Where I am getting at is, don't allow for one incident to be the reason you can't go near water. Sometimes we put ourselves in positions where we expect something to be a certain way only for it to be a different outcome than what we intended to be. There are things that we can do to get past it. I may not ever be able to swim, but I can find ways to overcome what has happened to me.

Also in the summer I still enjoy going to the beach. I just refused to go anywhere that the water goes above my chest. I am open to learn how to swim for the record. The key is to know what it is that you really want and to know whether or not you are willing to make that sacrifice to get there.

Now life is much harder than that, but it is a must to start facing the things were afraid of to see what we are not. Secondly, you must face your fear because you may not be afraid of the water itself. It could be the possibilities of circumstances. We create this storyline in our minds as soon as something don't go accordingly. I didn't drown that day, but it was shocking and caught me off guard. Maybe if I would have just extended my arms and flapped my feet, I may have learned how to swim that day.

At that time I was afraid. Unfortunately there are going to be situations that take place in our lives without warning. You shouldn't allow that to hinder you. You have to make the best judgment in order to get you through that situation.

That time at the pool was my initial reaction. When you fear it's hard to see into the future. You simply wake up in fear because of your current placement. Fear holds us back and it plays mind games. We have to learn to defeat fear, but facing it is another obstacle that we must overcome to get rid of the negative thoughts within our mind. If you're afraid to seek help you're not living in life itself. Your mind is.

Lastly, be in the present moment and get out there because nothing in life is guaranteed. Find ways to overcome. At that time it may not seem as though you are progressing, but life is a journey. There are situations in life that happen for a reason and might come expectantly as well as unexpected. What we have to understand is that we are in a world that is not perfect. There will be times in life where God will allow you to face a situation for that season.

"Sometimes in life you have to find a time and place to reflect on the things you've encountered."

Have you ever been awake and you felt as though you were awoke in a dark place. I have experienced what it is to be in the dark. It feels like you're all alone with no one there to help you. When you're in the dark, it's hard to find light. It becomes a challenge because you become afraid of the unknown. It all starts from when you were a child; you don't want the lights off so you turn the night light on. No matter how old you are being in the dark is an unpleasant feeling. When you're an adult, you find ways to cope with the reality, not by choice. If there was a way to guarantee light when it becomes dark, suddenly life would be a walk in the park.

Unfortunately it doesn't work that way. When life gets hard sometimes we can't find the light. So how do we develop a plan to guarantee it? There's no plan for the inevitable. All we can do is take one day at a time because it's beyond our control. How do we get out of this? We start off by facing our fears.

Fear is the ultimate failure of most people's lives. It prevents us from being who we really are. It re-routes us from seeking what our true purpose is. Don't let fear get in the way. It will make your journey a lot harder than what it already is.

When you look for that light even when it's pitch dark, it is an indication that you are a step closer. Although it does not feel like that, you just continue to move forward. Before you know it, you'll actually start to see the signs that there is a way out. We get afraid because we don't see the light at the end of the tunnel so instead of just taking a chance to walk through it we stay in that one exact spot.

If we have the courage to just continue to move in motion; even if it's not much, you'll be one step closer. Having faith that you will get there is your pass to freedom. It is not fair to you to have to carry weight that you may not understand. Don't be a prisoner when you have the option to be free. Having a gift of a complex mind is a blessing in itself. So I say keep searching because you are oh so worth it. This will become easier as time passes, but don't make darkness in life last forever. I felt like I never would get out of darkness. It feels like a permanent place even though it's not where I wanted to be.

Learning how to escape can feel like a full time job. It's time and dedication that you have to put forth before you can escape. Having an understanding is helpful but in order to apply them you have to be willing and also have the ability. *"As long as you're breathing you are able."* Just believe that you can do it. Have faith and humble yourself.

"When you believe in yourself, things will naturally gravitate towards you."

My battle with anxiety worsened as I became more aware of myself. I realize all the things that I have been through, I just replayed thoughts over and over again until I became sick. I became accustomed to feeling sick and the only way that I could cure myself was through abuse. I could remember so many

69

experiences that I felt when I was in a really dark place and it didn't feel good.

All I wanted to do was sleep and when I looked at myself I saw no hope. I let people treat me like I was nothing. I also treated myself like I was nothing. I lost so much faith in myself. I was in and out of relationships.

I never felt any satisfaction and many of my relationships I could never feel satisfied because no one could understand the battle that I was going through because it was within. I wanted the other person to understand the frustration that I had within myself. I was so unhappy because as I was going through the storm I focused on who I was at the time.

You have to get out of focusing on the person that you are currently and focus on the person that you are becoming. I felt that what I saw in the mirror was the finished product of me. You have the ability to change your reality. What I realized was that the people who are in my life weren't hurting me and they weren't the enemy. The true enemy was inside me. You have to admit that you are the enemy and stop blaming others. It all starts with you!

The relationships that I chose to be in put so much stress on myself. When I was 15 years old I got pregnant with my first child. It was so hard for me. I was a single mother, my daughter's father refused to be there and I had to figure out a way to provide for my daughter. At this time I just knew that I had so much to figure out in my life. I just knew that I would get pregnant and be with this man for the rest of my life. It didn't happen. In fact I became a single mother right after I gave birth to my daughter.

I remember having a job and the struggle that I had to go through just to get to work. I mean it was literally a struggle! I would walk through the pouring rain with my daughter in one hand, and an umbrella in the other hand. While she cried because she was getting wet, I cried because of my frustration with my situation. In the winter, I also carried my daughter through the snow to the bus stop. I could just remember the snow going up into my boots and getting stuck, I continued to walk in the snow as I tried to pull my foot out while tripping as I walked with her.

I would ride the bus to my job, sitting at the door by the exit with my daughter in her car seat while customers walked by, looking at this young girl who had a baby. I would feel so uncomfortable and embarrassed at how people looked at me as if I had made the worst mistake or committed some type of crime. My mother would meet me there to get my daughter and I would then start work. At this time I can remember the frustration I felt had put so much responsibility on my soul being a young mother. I remember feeling unworthy like I wouldn't amount to anything because I was a mother at a young age. I felt disgusted. I just thought people had no respect for me.

None of my friends had kids and I felt like a loner. I could say that I always had some kind of ambition because through the storm I still wanted more for myself. Deep within I knew that the person I saw was more than. I tried my best to be this perfect young mother. I knew I needed some work on myself. I was so ashamed of myself, ugly and disgusted. I hated my life.

My mother tried to help me the best way that she could, but it just wasn't enough. It wasn't the life that I expected for myself. There are places that we get to in life and may not understand how we got there. Trying to understand becomes draining. The best thing to do is take one day at a time. I always ask myself what am I doing to deserve this. Why do I attract this type of energy in my life? Why am I not attracting wonderful men to help me become a better person or wonderful friends that I can hang out with? These were wonderful circumstances that felt unreachable. I would look at other people's lives and couldn't understand why my life had to be so miserable.

I started resenting myself and it

wasn't the fact that I couldn't even stand up to the things that I felt I deserved. You have to be willing to stand up for what it is that you want by not settling. I wanted so much for myself and I just didn't understand why I couldn't get it. The doubts that I had within myself were endless. We have to learn that that rough drafts are our platform.

"Even when it's dark, there's light at the other side."

I carried a lot of weight through my teenage years. I had to start to fighting for myself. I realized that when you're fighting for yourself, you have changed so much more than relying on others to fight for you. I wanted somebody to fight for me. I wanted somebody to show me that they believed in me because I didn't believe in myself. I felt that my circumstances, my childhood, the choices, the mistakes and my flaws wouldn't allow me to be happy.

Don't wait for someone else to create that change. You have to be willing to make that change for yourself. It is okay to have help or input from other people, but in the end it is up to that individual to make that final decision. So every day I started working on myself more and more. I told myself that one day I'm going to get it right. I would not allow myself to be walked over because of the way that I perceived myself.

I have to find a way to reform my way of thinking.

"I had to take action because there was too much procrastination in my life."

My life still has darkness in it. It is different as you become aware. Your perception changes because I used to look at darkness as a disadvantage. You may feel that your life isn't what you wanted it to be or thought that it should be. I want to remind you that we don't choose our situation but God has the ability to get you out. Darkness could feel like a place that is permanent. I felt that it was a place that I wouldn't be able to come out of. If you are able to come out of a situation that has been brining you down that is God's favor.

When I experience darkness now, I look at it as an opportunity. Darkness should be used as motivation to find light because there will be sunshine in the morning. I just want you to know that even though there's darkness in those moments. When you look back at your life, you'll be able to look back and see how much you have grown. We can't erase our past. We can't erase where we are in this present moment.

All we can do is move forward and let go of the things that hurt us in the past. It is important to reflect and look back because you don't want to bury your pain. However, our life isn't a piece of paper. If we keep going back, trying to erase what has happened in our life, rewriting what ifs, erasing and writing over again, are we ever going to get to the end? We can't focus on perfection. The more that we focus on perfection instead of embracing the ugly, we begin to lose sight of the actual goal.

When we have a rough draft we scribble, we highlight and we underline, draw bubbles and write notes. Then we crumble the paper up and start over. Then we crumble it again, open it back up and then give up. Why give up after you have been working so hard. Although life isn't as simple as paper, we make all of the possible corrections aiming towards perfection. What if we took those same rough drafts; the ones that you have been underlying, adding marks on it, then we open up the crumbled paper and just lay them on the table and work through it.

Isn't it a lot more satisfying than just throwing it all the way? Nothing in life is perfect! The imperfection of that paper is what creates a beautiful one. It is about actually submitting the paper, the finished product. It is not about how many ugly marks you had to put on that paper. It is not about the ugly tears you had over your face through the process. When you submit yourself to God and allow him to see our ugly and we repent, we then open up the doors to eternity- a life of everlasting peace of mind.

God will give you unimaginable strength. How would you know if something is beautiful if you never allowed it to manifest? Trust in him and He will pull you through your weakest moments. We look at ourselves and because we see so many imperfections, we give up. We try to cover them up. They're called flaws to most people. I don't believe there's a thing such as a flaw.

"Every Little thing about us is what makes us beautiful. We just have to learn how to get through things by healing the empty spaces in our hearts."

Formation

"Envision The Person That You Want To Become."

When you're trying to condition your life into something new, you also have to become a new product of self. You have to be willing to use your product and maximize what you already have embedded in you. I think that everyone has a dream whether or not it's realistic or may seem like it cannot come true. Anything that you put your mind to can and will be fulfilled as long as you believe and work hard for it.

Formation isn't based on appearance,

it's within the mind. This is an important message because the new you with a new mind may not align with what you see. What you see isn't the finish product of what you think.

Learn how to condition your thoughts to the person you are called to be in spite if you're feeling loss of hope and feel like you're giving up on yourself, you have to be strong. The key word is feeling! Feelings come and they go! It is about having a true knowing of what you believe in. Your thoughts create the reality that you believe is to be true. Please don't get lost in feelings because you will become bitter, angry and resentful. Pain is poison and it will eat you at the core if you don't take care of it.

Being strong takes a lot of courage.

Faith is the medicine for the hurt that we experience in life. I was at a point in my life when I felt that I didn't have the ability to move forward in life. I was so afraid of the unknown. I wasn't sure where life was going to lead me. Life will present us with many things. Attempting to understand everything with such a complex mind is hard. When you don't have control over it, it becomes overwhelming. Remember that anything in life is possible.

If you dream big, then go hard for what you want. It's important to walk towards that vision you see. The power in having a vision is insurmountable. Having the opportunity to see what you want in life opens up the door to possibilities. How many times have you said today is going to be the last day I screw up or try to do something. Personally from my own experience I have done it on several occasions because I'm being "lazy" with depression.

There is no comparison. Depression varies from one person to the next. Some people face depression for multiple reasons. For example some become depressed about their circumstances, a loss of a loved one, loss of a job, abuse, etc. When trying to change, it is a challenge. When you're used to a certain way of thinking, how can you view anything from a different perspective? Trying to do something you never done before can make you doubt yourself. Personally I have doubted myself on many occasions because I was scared. Fear got in the way.

You may start wondering who am I? Where do I belong? You can instantly begin feeling out of place. When you have an imbalance within your mind or in your life, it counteracts with your daily life. The reality of your life is like an imbalance because you're battling daily. I think if you're at a point in your life in overcoming the obstacles you've encountered, it is time for a transition.

It is time to get used to the person that you transitioning into. The only way you can do that is by believing in yourself. When you believe in yourself, you feel better. When you feel better, you become more aware of yourself. People will see the change and you can be a positive influence in the lives of others.

I've realized that through my life I had been so angry about things I didn't understand without any explanation. Feeling angry about my past and bitter, I became frustrated with my

85

mind. I wanted a new mind because it was so hard to cope. We don't always have the answers. It's inevitable. Even though you are suffering, you have to find ways to get assistance with guidance. You have to figure out what it is that you want. I wanted a new mind because I couldn't get over the way I processed information in my mind. I decided I needed more.

I used faith to move forward. It is impossible to move forward because you'll basically accept anything when you're unsure of what will make you happy. I prayed that God gave me a renewal of my mind. Sometimes we don't know what makes us happy until we go through the worse. Also we can be in the best place and forget how it felt when we were at our worse. Not only do you prepare yourself physically, but also taking into consideration of changes mentally and physically will get you further. I think that when you're willing to admit that you need guidance, is a step forward to change.

When I was twenty five, I took the initiative and went to meet with a therapist because I knew that I needed someone in my life that was more knowledgeable than I was at the time. This was the first step towards my formation because I wanted more for myself. I didn't allow my pride to prevent me from seeking help.

You have to be willing to change other things in your life as well; whom you hang with, places you spend time; a job, a goal you want to accomplish and letting go of certain habits etc. I was at a point in my life where my life was moving at such a fast pace. I couldn't get a grip on what I was doing or where I was heading. Life started to hit me and I went into denial. It's hard to admit to yourself that you're failing. It was horrible. Not only was I suffering from depression, but also with the fact that I was a single mom and did not have a job or money to support them.

I had so much pain within and couldn't express it verbally. I carried the emotion within me and eventually it became my norm. I had to wear a mask. I'm very certain people sensed it. The mind is like an ongoing downloader. It downloads everything that has been inputted. Your brain will act in the same way if you put too much information in your mind all at the same time.

When we look at the computer it looks

perfect, especially if you have a MacBook. I'm not a phone lover, but somehow I learned to adapt. We expect the computer to function at all times. However, a computer can handle storage until it eventually crashes. I covered my pain with partying and drinking because it felt exciting, but it wasn't fun. I started to turn into a person I didn't know, nor how to confront or look at. I was disgusted with myself internally.

Are you happy with the life you have? Most people are concerned with how they look physically. The important thing is to look good internally and it will shine through you. I wanted internal beauty. So I started working on myself for the better. I can't say that I'm always happy with everything because there will be disappointments. It is what you do with the disappointment that makes a difference. If we allow the disappointment to take control of the person we want to become, it creates a pathway of continuous dissatisfactions. When you begin working on yourself for the better, it may feel uncomfortable. People aren't accustomed to it so they become reluctant without understanding.

"Objects don't give you harmony, peace within does."

As I wrote this book, I formulated new ways of thinking and developed new habits as well. I strived to be happy. I believed that transitioning is the hardest task. When I started becoming more aware of who was there for me, I slowly started eliminating people who weren't allowing me to grow mentally, physically, emotionally and spiritually. They were slowing me down and nothing was going right in my life. There are people who will come into your life and stunt your growth. You have to know when to pull out of a situation that is keeping you down.

I remember that I applied to a great college and got denied.. At the time it wasn't meant for me. When you think that you are being left behind, it is an indication that changes are waiting to be made. When I began to change, the people around me started to change. When you decide to pull yourself out of situations that is hurting you is when you develop growth, but the longer you decide to stay you suffer. When you learn how to get out, you change your position entirely. You will experience life's beauty.

I wrote the Dean of the school and

requested for the school to reconsider my application. I felt that I had the capabilities to achieve a Bachelor's Degree. I told myself that I would never give up on my dream. Within the next few weeks I got accepted into college. I was filled with so much joy. In that moment I told myself that I want to change my life. I didn't want to blame others for my circumstance. Formation is about getting through the storm and self-reflection. I had to face my battles everyday and I'm sure you do also, but remember there are so many ways to make that change. It all starts with you.

If you have a dream, go after it because you're worth it. Being a self-starter is by far not an easy job. It takes a lot of practice, but it's possible. You have to be willing to change things in your life that is keeping you back from

everything that you want in life. Through the
formation, I battled with myself. I realized that I
had to fight because I wanted to change
other's lives through my testimony. I believe
that it is important to know that you are worth it,
even when you feel you're at your weakest
point. You have to fight through it. You have to
keep fighting until you can't fight anymore.

When your mind is constantly going, you
fill it with things that were never there to begin
with. Once your mind feeds off the energy, you
can't allow your mind to function that way. It
will feed off the negative thoughts and your
positive ones will become poison. I had
struggled for a very long time. I woke up just
wanting to have a clear mind; with no clutter
because it was a lot to consume. I'm in and out
with a million things on my mind, creating new

projects, trying to figure out the changes that had to be made. I figured out that I could no longer keep replaying the tape: *"Why my life was the way it was?"* Dwelling on it kept me in one place.

If you are willing to go through the formation in your life, there will be many changes and surprises that take place. What I found helpful was realizing that God could do all things exceedingly and abundantly above all we can ask for. I also engaged in positive affirmations. For example telling yourself that you are great, that you can make change and that your life is precious can make all of the difference. Reminding yourself that you can do anything you set your mind on is also gratifying.

Setting goals is a great way for you to

see what you want to get out of life and to focus on one goal at a time. You should have a goal in my mind. You may not know the exact steps to get there, but if you start somewhere, you'll be a step closer. What I found challenging for me was focusing on too many goals at one time. My suggestion to you is to find one thing that is most important to you and focus on it. Work on it each and every day and once you become better then you can probably add one more goal and work at as well.

I used to be afraid to live my life and chase my dreams because I knew that it would be a lonely journey. Sometimes in order to get ahead you have to be willing to make changes. Remember that God won't give you too much that you cannot handle. When we work on too many things at one time, it becomes too much for one person to bear. I wanted to work on so many projects, a book, a movement, poetry, school and work. All of these goals are huge, but we have to find ways to break down each goal. For example, if there's something that you want to accomplish focus on that one thing by prioritizing, which will alleviate some of the pressure of you feeling overwhelmed.

Formation also comes with adaptation! There are situations that we face that can happen expectantly. During formation you have to be willing to develop a plan that aligns with what it is that you want in life. A lot of times we want to transform, but are not willing to adapt. Adaptation is an action and a process of adapting by choice or being adapted by particular circumstances, situations or a position that you are in. If you are not willing to take action you will become stagnant because overall it is a process. It will take a lot of effort and courage because depending on where you are in your life, you can become adapted to negative habits. If that is the reality, the deeper that you are adapted, the harder it will be to get adapted to positive things.

We spend a lot of our time thinking. We think about different things in the possibilities, regrets, work, family, finances, social life and so many other topics. It can become overwhelming. So how do we transform that? We do it by acceptance. I had a hard time accepting myself. When I looked at myself in the mirror I didn't think I could transform. I doubted myself way too much. I didn't accept anything about myself. I wanted to change everything because my mind did not align with my reality. Don't get caught up on what you feel that your life could have been or should have been.

Many people have suffered and probably been through worse. Stop feeling sorry for yourself and let God help you embrace everything that you have been through. It will be impossible to grow if you keep holding your life hostage. You don't want life to live you, but you want to live life because you're worth it. It is difficult to transform your life when you are stuck in one place. It will be difficult to embrace the season that your life is in if you are stuck in a season that has already passed. Having patience is also key!

Formation doesn't happen overnight. Formation is the little steps that we take to get to a greater purpose in life. Growing up I had no patience what so ever. I became sick over time. I was dissatisfied with everything and I became bitter and angry towards the life that I had. I hated the skin that I was in. I was so disappointed with everything I had been through up until this point. If you are dissatisfied, remember that formation is a process, but you have to be willing to be patient.

"Formation starts with realizing that we are always growing. You always are forming new ideas, new ways of thinking and different obstacles inevitably."

Compelling Allure

The Unexpected

"Be Prepared For The Unexpected"

I created the title of this chapter before it actually occurred. In 2016, I began writing this book. I developed the chapters based on my personal experiences. How was I aware of the inevitable or was it that I expected the unexpected? I always say be prepared for the unexpected.

I woke up that morning, just a few days after I found a great job opportunity. It was a job that I wanted for years. I was feeling depressed and lost. I had to resign from my job prior because my car got totaled. I wasn't ready for what was about to happen, but I had to prepare myself and knew that I needed to keep striving.

I prayed and prayed and I asked God to guide me. I also asked if He could take some of the weight off of my shoulders. Now that I have been offered a job, I could see my life changing for the better; more money to help provide for my kids and myself. I said to myself, *"Yes, my life is heading in the right direction!"* I felt that I finally was getting ahead. Then I got that call at seven in the morning on February 7, 2017. I was in the middle of getting my kids ready for school. This is when my life would take a huge turn.

The phone was ringing and I answered. I just thought it was another silly call from my cousin. He was always making ridiculous jokes. I was in for some shocking news.

He asked if I had spoken to my O'ma (great-grandmother). I said no, why? He bluntly told me the worse news of my life that I would never imagine receiving. The way that I received it was with no remorse, no sympathy.

"Brian got killed last night." In that instant moment I started to dream my hands, arms, legs and feet felt so numb. I felt like I was put in a freezer for that moment and reality hit. My body began to un-thaw with a tingling sensation as I grasped for air. In a matter of seconds, I started to scream to the top of my lungs like the cry of a newborn baby out of the womb. I felt like I was dying. I was given the worse news someone could ever experience; finding out that my baby brother was murdered.

At this time Brian was twenty-five years old. The way the news was presented to me, everything felt like dream. I couldn't move. I wanted to rewind everything. The thoughts I had, my inner voices telling me the worse and reminding of all the regrets I had. I hadn't spoken to my brother in over ten months. I remember the day I left Atlanta, GA, the week of my Birthday in 2016, he told me that he loved my crazy self. He told me to keep my head up and stay strong.

During the trip there was chaos. I hadn't seen my brother in years. It was unfortunate that we had a relationship built on distance due to our situation. At the age of nine I found out for the first time that I actually had a brother. It was a true surprise. I was too young to understand the situation fully, but I knew that I had a sibling and that was enough. Apart from this when I met my brother in person for the first time, it was relieving. I knew that there was always something missing in my life. All along it was my brother. However we tried our best to get past the lies and confusion from the family.

We promised each other that we would create the life that we felt we deserved as brother and sister. It had been almost twelve years since I had last seen my brother. I did not know that would be the last time I would hug him. So how do you recover from horrific traumatic situations? How do we get through the obstacles we are faced with?

As I sit here, I am grieving trying to overcome the pain, waiting for a breakthrough. I am oppressed within. I am drowning in my own flesh. How could I be blessed with a new job and instantly my life takes a turn? I had orientation the week of my brother's funeral. It was truly a dream that I was experiencing. I hadn't talked to my brother. Although we weren't talking over something petty, God gave me a revelation that he had to distance us because he wanted to protect me emotionally. My brother meant the world to me and I could never picture life without him in it.

I began to search plane tickets because I had to fly into North Carolina. His funeral was being held in South Carolina. Through the process of looking, I was in disbelief. It didn't feel like I was preparing for a funeral, it felt more like prison. I had little motivation and some faith, but I couldn't swallow the pill of knowing that I was going on a vacation that would impact me tremendously for the rest of my life.

When I arrived at the airport it was an

experience that I couldn't understand at the moment. I went to buy breakfast and I couldn't access my money. I had called my bank and expressed my concerns. At that time I was starving and I couldn't function properly. I spoke to a customer service representative and she saved me from losing my composure. I was frustrated but she made sure that I could access my money by going above and beyond for me.

Soon after I went to wait for my flight. I waited for about 30 minutes when I came to a realization that there was no plane and no one was boarding.

At this time I caught the attention of an employee and he explained to me that the plane left. I just knew that there was a possibility that I wouldn't make it to NC. Then something came over me. I had faith in the employee. He brought me over and explained the situation to the representative for boarding. The representative asked me what happened. At this point I knew that I was being tested and needed to humble myself.

I told him that I missed my flight and that there was construction going on in the area, which confused me. He looked at my original ticket, which was a connecting flight. He printed me out a new boarding pass for a straight flight. I felt blessed and was reminded that God wouldn't let me down. Once I arrived in Fayetteville, NC, I felt a sense of relief.

I thought my Valentine's Day would be different. I was standing in front of a church; my body shivering and shaking as I saw his body raised above the casket. I instantly became weak, feeling as If I am going to collapse. I am so confused. As I gained strength from God, I began to walk down the aisle. As I get there, I see how beautiful he looks. He looked so peaceful. I kissed him as if I was giving him a kiss good night.

In life we are faced with the unexpected. When trying to prepare for it, things aren't as intense until you're actually expected to face the experience. In order to be strong, it takes courage and confidence. The loss of my brother has been an eye opener. I feel required to do everything in my power to live out his legacy. The pain we feel sometimes feels like it lasts forever. If you take a moment and confidently believe that you can surpass the obstacle, you will.

We have to remember that it's temporary. Pain is temporary. It comes and goes. Don't get caught up in your mind and keep fighting. Don't get caught up in your feelings and keep striving. Suffering from mental health, depending on the extent, sometimes distorts our mind, but we must defeat it. You have to stay strong and be willing to move forward. Don't allow your mind to get stuck in the moment. I found myself getting sick over time, because I over thought everything and it took a toll on me.

Life hits us with so many situations and it could feel overwhelming. I know you're wondering, how did you overcome the pain? Well sadly you don't, it comes and it

"All we can do is learn how to cope with it."

goes. I thought there was a magical way to get rid of pain.

The fear of the unknown is the largest barrier for most. When you're unsure what life has to offer you, it results in making more mistakes trying to figure it out rather than what is right in front of you. If we took what was right in front of us instead of dwelling on what it may be, you would enjoy life a lot more. Unfortunately, there is not a guaranteed way for us to know what the outcome of our lives would be.

There are always things that are going to happen unexpectedly whether it's flat tire, loss of a loved one, getting laid off, going through a divorce and etc. However, it is how you view the unexpected life events. You can allow it to make you or break you.

It's unfortunate that we do not know these things are coming. I'm not saying look for the worst. It's about looking at what's right in front of you. Nothing in life will last forever, but while it's here you must enjoy it.

Yes the possibilities may come in your mind, along with doubts and fear, but we cannot allow that to hinder us from our happiness. All these factors affect many lives. Instead of taking chances people often stay in one spot wondering if they took the chance. It is the same as taking a chance, but actually doing it. Whether or not you take a chance, you are putting yourself through the same amount of anxiety wondering.

Don't let fear of the unknown stop you from exploring life. You have to go through different things to get to a place that is destined for you to be. If I had not gone through the many challenges that I faced, I would not have been able to share with you the many stories that made me stronger.

Sometimes we go through things in life without understanding. In the midst of it you can lose hope. I've been where I lost hope. I started to examine every negative experience and quality of my life. If you become fixated on it, you will become depressed. It is okay to have self-reflection because it allows you to look at yourself more deeply. But it's unhealthy when you give yourself negative self-talk. You want to be able to give yourself positive affirmation in spite of everything that you

"The more you give yourself positive affirmation even when things happen beyond your control; you begin to have a sense of inner peace."

have gone through.

I don't feel that there is anyone in this world that enjoys the unexpected, unless it's something that happens and has a positive influence. Ultimately the feeling of uncertainty can be mind boggling. Not knowing how you're going to get past a day due to a sudden illness through a loss of a loved one, loss of a job, divorce, etc. The most important thing is that you have to realize that in life things are always going to happen.

No matter how hard we try to prevent things from happening, inevitably it does. Having acceptance of the obstacles that we face in life will allow you to see the positive out of any negative encounter. In order for me to stay above surface, I constantly had to remind myself that I am worthy and that God is always in the midst of everything.

God does not want to punish anyone. He wants us to be humble, because He will work things out for the better. It is not the things that we see that guarantee the promise that God has over our life. It is the things that we don't see because God is always making a plan for the betterment of our lives. Throughout our journey, we try to control our path and when one unexpected thing happens in our path, things may take a shift.

If you were to look back and say, *"Had this not happen I would or wouldn't be here in this situation."* Within my personal experience, I think that if it did not happen, where would life have led you? Even though we face the unexpected, it does not mean that our journey is over. On a faith based perspective, it is that

God puts us in these situations to position ourselves. Sometimes we need to be redirected with where our internal goals take us because it may be an alternative route that will put us back on the route so we can begin to see things differently. It is hard to bounce back when unexpected things happen in life. Think about it. If you got angry every time you put a destination into your GPS and Siri redirected you; you wouldn't be happy especially if you travel daily.

I went on a trip to Virginia in August 2018. The GPS re-routed my mother maybe three or four times on our way there and back. What my mom couldn't understand was why it continued to do that and she had become frustrated. Instead of her continuing to drive, she found herself turning around to try to put herself on the right path. This is similar to how we may handle things in life. Sometime we think we're on the right track and we get redirected. Sometimes we end up doing the things that we feel is the right things to do. We look at what is right in front of us and we start to make plans. Sometimes we have to be redirected and it could open up new opportunities. It could also lead us to a path that is right for us.

I had to realize in my life that the plan I had for myself were completely different than the plan that God had for me. We also may be on the wrong track and be at a standstill. The great thing about traveling is that the GPS isn't our only resource. Sometimes God could be directing us to avoid a certain path for a reason. What I have found useful is not to question it but to keep moving forward. In life it's similar as we become stabilized. We depend on electronics because of the convenience. We don't realize that there are so many other resources available such as a map, signs and compasses. In life we become dependent on particular resources and if we get lost along the way, we don't know which way to turn.

The first thing that I turn to when I feel is stuck is God. If you aren't religious, you may turn to something else that helps redirect you. It could be family, friends, etc. I think having faith no matter what is key.

I put my faith in God. I believe that as long as I have Him in my heart, I will work with him as He will work with me. In life, it's not going to always be smooth sailing. Sometimes we're going to get redirected. It is up to us to

have a positive mindset in order to continue the

journey that God has put us on.

———————————————

"Follow your internal GPS because it's the number one thing you can trust."

———————————————

Compelling Allure

Reality

"Don't Become Complacent"

Nothing in life is perfect, as cliché as that may sound. I lived my whole life trying to make my life perfect. I came to the realization that your mind isn't perfect and nothing around you will be close to it. I woke up one day and realized that I have been suffering for so long. What was different on this day is that I woke up with so many regrets.

I had one of the worst arguments with my mother. I said the most hurtful things that anyone could ever say to a person. In that moment I was trying to hurt her because she hurt me. I told her that if she raised my brother and I so well, then why is my brother dead?

I didn't feel the hurt by saying that until

the next day when I sobered up. Instantly I felt like taking my own life. I didn't want to live anymore. I love my brother dearly. Because he was murdered, I have pain living inside of me. I don't have any excuse behind what I said to my mother. I admit that we were both intoxicated, but I will not use that as justification for my actions.

In the past my mother and I have bumped heads. We have always had some kind of tension in our relationship. The one thing that we do have in common is that we love each other. How do you mend a relationship back together that has been broken repetitively? I found myself repenting to God. I had to reveal my ugliness to Him. I had to acknowledge the fact that I was emotionally, physically and mentally disturbed.

When you find yourself in this place, you truly have a responsibility. This is nothing but the ability to respond to someone or something. Your response to anything in life will truly have an impact on how you view things as well as the journey that you will be on.

Everyone has the ability to respond. It is up to you on how you want to do it. You can respond negatively or you can respond positively. The ball is in your hand. A little advice, never hold grudges. Even if you can't forget the pain that you caused someone or the pain you endured.

Do not judge, and you will not be judged. Do not condemn and you will not be condemned. Forgive and you will be forgiven. Matthew 6:37

Trying to find a balance isn't always easy. But it is important to find out a way to manage. If not, it can affect you tremendously. I wish that I could change what happened between my mother and I. Unfortunately that's not how life works. In life there are things that happen inevitably. How we think and respond dictates our next step in life. It is the foundation of your true reality.

My thoughts have played a major role in my life. The ones that hurt me the most were the negative ones. I allowed myself to make them come alive because I became accustomed to them. When a drug addict goes through withdrawals, they immediately need a fix. That is similar to how the mind works. I had been used to negative thoughts because of the negative things that took place in my life.

Therefore, leaving me no other option, I had to come up with my own solution. The solution was of course a bad one. I was unstable within my thoughts. I found myself arguing, having many mood swings and dissatisfied with almost everything when I experienced withdrawals. I became an addict myself.

Then I finally reached a point where it didn't help. So then I had to increase my dose. This led to unhealthy relationships, alcoholism and poor choices. I did not try hard enough to make better choices. When I felt things were going right in life, I was happy! Then I would reach a point where I felt things weren't really changing. The closer I got to change, the further back I fell. I began walking backwards due to fear. I would try to convince myself that things would eventually change in my life such as my circumstances, my mind and ultimately me!

I thought I would one day wake up and be a different person. I wanted instant gratification. I then realized that eventually things would manifest. It is important to continue to do the right things because if something is going to happen on God's watch, then you have to believe that He is your Protector.

"As long as you strive for the best that you can be, is when you'll reach your fullest potential."

I can't begin to explain how my reality didn't align with the person that I was aiming to be. I think that is the most frustrating and discouraging part, when you know that you

126

want to change and want to be the person you envision yourself as. This is the best time to sit back and reflect on the things that aren't allowing you to grow. I have been through more ups and downs then I ever could imagine.

I believe that we are constantly in a dark place when we obsess over the reality of how circumstances are, but you can't become complacent. The more that you sit there and stay in one spot; it is what makes it difficult to get up and go. Sometimes we need that push because it is not easy when you struggle mentally.

In reality I know that I am a smart, loving and a caring person. I never allowed a diagnosis to determine who I am as a person. Don't allow someone's judgment of who you are to shape you. Instead use it as motivation. I have met people who have struggled with depression, anxiety, and other mental health disorders. What I have learned about myself is to not beat myself up about the pain I had inside.

The problem is that it wasn't always only my pain. I carried others' pain that made me sick internally. Everyone has a different way of coping. Some people smoke, drink, drugs; have sex, eat obsessively and many more habits. I can't describe the moments when I felt I couldn't tolerate anything around me. Anyone who has depression is a case-by-case situation. My true reality is that I took the initiative. I said that I wanted to kill myself over 100 times.

I have been through really tough

hardships that are difficult to talk about. However, your story could be someone else's blessing. The struggles that many people go through sometimes don't have a voice. I had a friend who came out of jail and was trying to change his life around. He did 10 years in prison for a rape that he did not commit. When he told me this, I believed in him. I had faith.

We had continuous conversations about it. He was a God-fearing man. He always prayed for me. He did this day in and day out. We laughed together, cried together. One of the biggest pains that he had was the stigma of rape that he had hanging over him. The way he described it was hurtful for me to see and hear, but only he truly knew how that pain felt.

Oftentimes people are caught up on the superficial aspects of life. It's when you really pay attention and apply yourself for the better, which is not an easy thing to do. I always tried to encourage him. But then it got to a point that our friendship fell apart. We both weren't happy about a lot of different things. I got a call from a woman who asked to speak to me. I'm not sure what was happening, but I knew it was nothing good. The woman, who is my friend's mother, told me that her son was found dead in his bed. The news destroyed me. The ups and downs that we went through all went down the drain. It is when I had seen the reality of life.

We have a lot of forces behind the way we think, choices that we make etc. I have not made the best choices, but I have made the worse ones. So how do we break out of this cycle? Some people choose to do things that aren't healthy. Some people take their own lives or even others mentally, physically or emotionally. It is hard to have a stigma. Even when I would hear my doctor say that I'm depressed, I had a problem with it. Just like my friend did. He wanted society to believe that he was normal, that he did not rape anyone. Yet he couldn't get his point across.

It is difficult to face yourself when you think of what people may think of you, if you told them that you were depressed. That intimidates people and puts fear into your heart. No one wants to be judge with a negative connotation. My purpose is to help you understand how mental health affects everyone. It is one of the industries that is growing all over the world. There are alternatives being intentional going through the pain, hurtful thoughts, having regrets, taking accountability, researching, writing thoughts down, working out, eating healthier, changing your surroundings and embracing life for what it is.

It sounds so easy, but it's not. I have struggled to get to this point where I am. You get to a point where you're tired. That is the best time to reflect on your life, mind, body, and spirit. It's not until you reach that point. Everyone has their own timing, but the harsh reality is if we don't take the time to put the work in how do you reach your full potential? The solution for me is a number of things.

I looked for a church that I instantly gravitated to because it felt right. Going to church rebuilt my faith and strength in myself and also others around me. What has helped me so far is being intentional and doing the things that truly matters, according to my therapist. He taught me to do the things that matter to me, including finding things that bring me healthy joy. Choosing a therapist was the first step for me to get moving. I honestly feel in my heart if I were not consistent with going, I would not have opened up opportunities for myself.

"Pain gives us fear, which blocks us from the possibilities."

It is the greatest feeling when your hard work pays off. Had I given up I would not be where I wanted to be. I had to give up on certain friendships and relationships. I also had to give up bad habits because it wasn't doing me any good. I started doing things that I felt would help me be the best version of myself. Create your reality by being intentional and doing what truly matters.

Of course things don't always go so smoothly in life. Circumstances change, we then change with those circumstances and that has an effect on our realities. I realized that no matter what path that we are on, we need to always have faith in everything that we do. When the hard times approach, is when we should be mindful, find the gratitude and seize that present moment.

The reality is that during difficult times determines how strong we really are. When things do not go according to your life, it does not mean that you should give up. In order to overcome the situations that we are faced in life, we must be patient. In the moments when we feel impatient, these are the true blessings in disguise. We don't realize that reality is when you have patience; you start to see things in a

134

different light. What I have learned in the process is that we create our reality based on how we perceive things in life. I am not here to tell you what to believe in.

My purpose is to share what has helped me get to a place of acceptance. When you are going through a storm, it is hard to find the positive things in those moments. It is not until you actually overcome the obstacles where you start to look back and reflect. Sometimes people do not have that opportunity. The only way to have that opportunity is by making an opportunity for yourself.

Every day you must show gratitude for one thing. You must be intentional. Oftentimes people spend their lives mapping out everything in their mind. What they're going to do. What their next move is going to be. How they're going to do it, but they never take the step forward towards what they are planning. This becomes a spiraling mess within the mind because there's just too much information that is not actually being output. Our mind is like a computer, when there is so much information being put into the computer eventually it crashes.

"You have to start to take out some of this information, so that you can make room for the things that are really important to us."

Your reality is now, but reality is also in the future. What my reality is now can change tomorrow. There's a difference between knowing and feeling. Do not allow your current situations to dictate what your future will be. It is so easy to get fixated on the situation that you are in right now. Remember hard times don't last forever. It is the people who take the time to self-reflect.

I figured out alternatives to reach your fullest potential. At one point in my life, the reality for me was that present moment. I allowed my reality to dictate my future, my next move, as well as my mind. You don't want to live that way. You don't want to live feeling stuck each and every day. I know what it feels like to wake up each and every day feeling stuck. I have experienced the same things that anyone else could have experienced in life. What I want you to realize is that we all have to face reality one day, but what are you going to do when it's your turn to be intentional.

When you are intentional, it takes you to

greater heights. Being intentional means that although you may have to be up for work by 6:30 a.m. You make a decision to wake up at 6 a.m. instead. That is being intentional. Every time that we are intentional towards something or someone, it benefits us in the present moment and in the future. We create habits over time and that becomes your norm. Over time it will no longer feel like a job. It will become part of you.

If you sit in your room, in the dark, underneath your covers, the reality is that it's dark and you're under the covers. What happens when it's dark beyond the covers? It is easy for your mind to drift away. You may feel down and completely hopeless. These are the moments where you are supposed to shift your mindset by taking a deep breath, meditate

138

on positive things and realize that the dark does not mean it will be forever.

Therefore, you should always try your best to think positive because the reality is the sun will come out in the morning. If you continue to make your reality dark, darkness will remain in your life. Even when the sun comes out, your reality will lead you to believe that the sun is not shining.

It is not always easy to face reality. The moral of this is that we have to work a little harder to embrace every moment. If you're sitting here and you feel like your reality is your circumstances are so bad that you don't have a way out.

"The only reason that I can give you this information is because I would like to remind you that I've been in the same places you have been."

I can

understand the frustration that you are feeling. In the previous chapters, I mentioned all the trials and tribulations that I faced. I shared this story with you because I don't want you to become a victim.- Life is short. Life is precious. Every day you have a chance to grow. So don't let your reality make you feel stuck. The truth is the reality is now. What is amazing about reality is that you have the power to change it, as long as you are able to respond.

Be intentional and figure out what you need to do to get to the next step in your life. It is unfortunate that some of us in this world have to fight so much harder than others. When you compare your life to others,

You see that it is so much easier. But that is just the exterior. We are all facing similar battles within the mind, whether it's stress, anxiety, depression, trauma, confusion, worry, desperation or loss of hope.

The only way that I was able to overcome many obstacles was by having faith and believing that I can change my reality every day. Instead of sitting there you have to get up. You just have to keep pushing and pushing yourself until you can't push no more. Don't allow your mindset to dictate your reality. Learn how to reform your mindset so that you can be intentional and do things that really truly matter in your life.

When you start to do the things that you truly want to do, you release so much clutter. It's like cleaning out a junk drawer, or your car trunk, or the basement.

Every time you remove something, you

create space. Your mind needs space, so

remember that you have to set a goal and you

have to master it.

> *"Whether that goal is waking up each and every day at 6; when you become a master at the little things, when the bigger things come in your life, and more opportunities become available to you, it'll be easy to persevere."*

Understanding

"Know Your Truth"

We have many different aspects to our life. It can cause a lot of pressure. I understand that I have been hurt, abused mentally, physically and emotionally. The pain that lived in me for most of my life was hard because it was without any true understanding as to why I felt this way. All I know is that it's one of the worst feelings ever, not knowing why you feel so hurt and destroyed from the inside out.

As I cried and started to think about the people who were in my life, I made calls and no one seemed to be around. The people who I thought cared about me treated me as if I'm the one who is always busy as to why they didn't reach out. So I thought about the conversations that my therapist and I had about reaching out to them. I started to practice. What I noticed were a lot of barriers for me to make plans with them. This left me feeling rejected and useless. I was left wondering why they didn't want to be bothered with me. I wondered what I was doing wrong.

Instantly a feeling of anxiety and hopelessness would overcome me. I decided at that moment to go into the bathroom. I opened up the prescription cabinet. I asked myself if I would commit suicide, would people care then? I instantly shut the cabinet and began to cry. I got on my knees and rebuked the devil. I prayed and asked God to remove the negative thoughts and actions while in the bathroom.

I stood up and looked at myself in the mirror. I noticed how swollen my face was from the crying. At that moment I was looking from the inside out because my mind was taking control. From that point of view I looked at myself and called myself pathetic. My father's voice came over me. He always says, *"There's no sense of you crying. You got to be strong. This is the real world and it's a lot of stuff that's going to happen."* He reassured me that life will not be perfect and that I will face many more obstacles, but I must remain strong.

I always tried to take heed of what my dad expressed to me. My father is my mentor, best friend and the best dad. I decided to go back into the living room. I practiced deep breathing and looked outside of myself, then looked at me from the outside in. I saw this beautiful, strong woman, a child of God; full of wisdom and strength from the man who uplifted my spirit. God!!! He made me realize that He needs me as much as I need Him. I began to look at the pictures of myself as if I was deceased.

I noticed how happy I looked, even though I portrayed to look happy because I had years of practice wearing a mask. As I mentioned previously, happiness is being intentional. I then began to look at pictures of my son and my daughter. I realized how blessed I am to have such beautiful kids and how devastated my daughter would be if I took my life. She is the oldest and that would have been a burden on her. I thought about all the pain she would encounter from not having two parents. Her father was absent most of her life.

146

I also thought about how my son would be hurt and grow up without a mother. I felt horrible. The importance of this is that when your suffering from any kind of pain whether it's due to life experiences or mental health, you can get lost in feeling like the world is against you. The beauty in all of it is that you began to have an understanding of your life by fighting for it. You can't give up! You reflect on your emotions by writing them down, making notes, expressing yourself to friends and family if you have any.

As I was working on this book, I got a text from an old friend who said, *"Hi Princess B!"* It felt so good! Instantly I felt like someone cared! He played a role in my life. He always believed in me and was also my manager at one point. He always gave me a chance. He understood my situation and helped in the best way he could. Apart from this as I was writing, I also got a call from my Aunt Deborah. Instantly she could hear in my voice that something was wrong. God is so good and will use people to do things in other people's lives in the midst of trouble.

With so much concern and urgency in her voice she asked, *"What's wrong?"* I explained to her that I was thinking about my brother. I had a lot on my mind. I didn't tell her the whole truth. However, the timing was perfect. I felt my body, mind and spirit return back to me. It's amazing how you can get lost that easily. That's why it's detrimental to understand that tough times don't last forever, but the strongest believers do.

"Don't make a long term decision that can change everything forever, because emotions are temporary."

If I would've made the decision to take my own life, I would not be able to share my story with the world. I'm being honest, because I am talking about the pain that I experienced at the time. I felt the true emotions that are lying within me at this exact moment. Love yourself and love others.

Create your reality and don't allow your thoughts to dictate the next step in your life. It's the power in being strong. We have to stay strong as individuals, whether young or old, male or female, white or black. The best way to develop an understanding of where you are in your life or where you should be is through confidence.

Confidence is overcoming your fears. A lot of us do not know what self -worth is. We either were taught or weren't, were treated unworthily or we had a difficult time accepting us. How can you understand where you are going, if you don't know who you are? How do you know who you are if you've never been introduced?

We must listen first to be understood. God gave us two eyes, two ears and one mouth. It is purposefully set up that way so that we see and listen. I don't think that we fully know who we are, but we can get a sense of understanding. My advice is to seek spiritual guidance that strengthens you as an individual. I have always been a believer that God was always with me. Although I didn't grow up in a church, I always tried to go with friends. I enjoyed it a lot because of the closeness. I didn't have much family. I was always home, and I wasn't allowed to stay at other people's house often. I always prayed as a little girl and always had lucid dreams about briefcases of money. I would wake up with hopes that it was still there.

I believe that this happened because even as a young girl, I wanted so much more out of life. As I got older, my dreams were surrounded by fear. I was running from something or someone, drowning, getting shot, losing someone, broken relationships, etc. I had experienced a difficult time in my life. I was twenty five and I became afraid of a lot of things. The number one thing was death.

I began to develop a way of thinking

that I had to get the work done before I died so that I could leave a legacy behind for my children. People would say that it isn't normal to think of things like that. I agree to an extent.

Everyone faces mid life crisis, anxiety and depression. It was my first year of college on the dean's list. I was eager to attend college and work towards my Bachelor's Degree. I wanted the best for my children and was working on achieving my goals. What made my experience different than others was that I could never let go of the thoughts until I had a panic attack at my mother's house. It was a life changing moment for me.

Before I knew it, my hands were deformed and locked due to the lack of oxygen I was getting to my brain. My mother was in shock and she couldn't dial the emergency line for 9-1-1. The kids were playing outside and I couldn't breathe. I remember in that vague moment feeling like that was it. I literally felt that I had spoken death over my life and that was it for me. In that moment I had to decide how bad I wanted to breath.

> *"Happiness is not genetic; it is something that you adapt to based on your environment, thoughts and actions. It is being Intentional."*

Everything I was building in 2015 was going to vanish because that day I thought I was going to be gone forever. Moments later there were many men standing around me telling me to breath. I began crying more when I realized that I wasn't dreaming. I remember the paramedics telling me to slow down my breathing. I remember saying my hands are stiff and locked. They encouraged me to breathe. They said that it was a result of my brain not getting oxygen, so they needed me to breathe. I didn't comprehend what was being said to me. I only remember feeling like I was going to die.

I remember my son was playing with a ball. When I thought he was going to run in the street after it, it gave me a panic attack. As I'm lying on the stretcher being brought to the ambulance, the feeling of nervous and anxiety started off strong. When I got into the truck, I felt vulnerable, which was a feeling I never felt before.

They were talking to me and taking my vitals. In that moment there was a beautiful

Caucasian woman. She almost appeared as an angel. She smiled at me and said, *"Everything is okay, were going to take care of you!"* She said it with a sincere tone of voice.

I began thanking God. I expressed to her what was going on. I told her that I'm a single mother and was determined to stay on the Dean's list. I also explained that I lived on my own with my two children, struggling to make ends meet. She praised me for my accomplishments and said that she wouldn't be able to do it. She then told me that I was strong.

When I was dropped off at the hospital I was more relaxed. That is when the doctor told me that I experienced an anxiety attack. I never knew that I had anxiety. The doctor explained that it could happen at any moment in our lives.

My point is that we can't predict the future. Trying to understand what was happening to me at that moment was impossible. It was a sign that I need to gain clarity of who I was, where I was heading and figure out what needed to be changed in my life.

"In order to gain control over one's life, you have to be willing to have patience for yourself."

Change

"Get Unused to the Old You"

You want to change, but change is scary. Your mind is telling you that you can't do it. I'm sorry to say, but the only way that you can change is by working hard. A lot of us do not want to work hard for it. The first step is you have to want to change. The second step is to figure out the things that are preventing you from working towards that change.

The third step is to understand your purpose of wanting to change. Only then can you envision what that change looks like. Finally when you do change, what do you plan on doing with that change?

It is important to know that change is going to be beneficial to you. Personally, change was hard for me. All I wanted to do was hang out with my friends, so that's exactly what I did.

When I was feeling stressed, I couldn't wait until Friday came around. Hold on, I couldn't wait until it was Tuesday. It was $2.00 Tuesday at the Russell in Hartford, Connecticut. Wednesday's were Russian Lady $10 wristband unlimited drinks until 12am; and Thirsty Thursdays were everywhere. Fridays were NV in Hartford Connecticut, Saturdays were the Cloud, Vibz, Uptown Hartford ,Connecticut and the Indian Social Club where there were special events.

This was my normal week, hanging out with my friends and going out spending money that I didn't have, drinking and being frivolous with life. I can admit my wrongdoings. The question is, are you willing to admit yours? You have to be willing to admit yours. In order to change you have to be real with yourself. When you look at yourself in the mirror, are you truly happy for the person you are looking at, on the inside and out. You may look at yourself thinking that you're the next Drake or Cardi B. There is nothing wrong with that because we all have an alter ego, however how do you feel inside?

When you look at yourself in the mirror, are you really happy overall. It is so easy to fall in love with how you look. This is called being conceited. When you are confident, it means that you accept the person that you are. We are all unique in our own ways. I cannot judge you and neither can anyone else. I did not write this book to tell you, *"15 ways To Change Your Life Now and Forever."*

I wrote this book to shed a light on individuals who feel that they are alone. I wanted to share this story with you to prevent people from giving up and losing hope. The obstacles that I have faced in life by far in the twenty eight years that I have been living are unimaginable. This book also isn't to tell you about my whole life or how you should live yours. I feel comfortable sharing this story with you to ensure that you are motivated to work towards your future. I want to be a part of changing your life for the better.

No matter how many battles that you have within your mind, no matter what situation that you are in right now, I want to help you believe that you can change. Change is so

scary because you never know what is going to

come next.

_____

"Why live your life sitting there and not taking the next steps towards change because you're so afraid."

_____

Unfortunately, fear is our greatest

setback. It prevents us from the only thing that

really matters to us. People who should be

doing something in this world become

stagnant. You're mind then starts to decline.

You have to do the things that you really don't

want to do. It is necessary to work towards all

of your goals because you have the ability to

respond. Continue to work hard and do not

give up on yourself by getting caught up in

negative ways of thinking. If you allow your

mind to take control of your life, you will lose your creativity. Before you know it, you'll forget the seeds that you planted.

If you go back and think about the things that made you happy it would bring positive energy to your soul. You can use those moments to help you get back to that point in your life. You'll be able to begin to identify those moments in your life when you felt happy and reflect on where you are currently.

It is hard to reflect, but it's even harder to start over after facing many obstacles. If you feel like you never been happy, it is truly possible to be. I didn't feel happy for a long time. The truth is some days are better than others. The beauty in it all is that I know hard times won't last forever. I have the ability to make a choice to decide to be happy. You also have the ability, even if you can't see it!

Even when you are suffering from depression, it may take additional steps, but the important thing is to be intentional. You may think happiness is not in here. You cannot swallow a pill of happiness. What you can do is seek happiness. Happiness is something that we have to find within ourselves and within our lives. Yes, it is hard work. Especially when you feel that you are alone in this world.

You have to find something positive that makes you happy whether it's cleaning, cooking, reading, and listening to uplifting music or motivational YouTube videos. I thought alcohol brought me happiness, but it only brought me temporary freedom. I thought that because I was free when I was drinking that it was my way to seek happiness. It wasn't until I created a negative reality. The process of change is so easy to get caught up in negative things.

Take your life seriously and be intentional. Remember where you came from and think about where is it that you want to head towards. Never give up on yourself and keep striving to greatness. Don't get caught in your past and remember that you are not perfect, but you will be forgiven. If you work towards betterment for yourself and loved ones, you will see what you began to attract.

When you change, there are many different levels. The key is to jump into it and try your best to submit yourself into a life that you deserve. Although you may not want to change and it may not feel like you need to, I believe that we all have room to grow. You never want to stop wanting to improve yourself

because you are profitable. Don't allow the lack

of change to depreciate your value.

"You must be intentional by guarding your eyes and your ears."

Compelling Allure

Now and Forever

"Make A Legacy"

How do we sustain a life that we are just beginning to understand? This is now, the present moment. What you do now will affect your forever. The obstacles that you face now will contribute to your future. The response to the obstacles will be the barriers that prevent you from reaching your forever. It is what you do when it's your turn. We live on purpose because we were put here to serve.

My belief is that God put me here and He kept me here to live on purpose. My purpose is to show you that you're not on your own. I understand that we all have our different obstacles whether they are big or small. I can't identify it because that would be bias. What I do know is that everyone has a different path. You have to be willing to focus on the one set for you. I know that it isn't easy, but it is essential.

Please don't get caught up on what you didn't have and what you should have had. What you have now and how you preserve it, it will determine your forever. How you perceive your now will make the true difference in your life. Your forever takes a lot of building. There are plenty levels. Don't allow your now to make you afraid and keep you hindered. Strive and walk with your head high. Your forever will last if you appreciate what you have right now.

If you can't appreciate your now, how do

you think you'll appreciate the future that God has already prepared although you can't see it now? Every time we doubt God because of what we don't see, we doubt His blessings He have over our lives and our future becomes forever gone. Fight and believe that there will be a breakthrough.

"Every Individual has their own discretion in regards to what he or she defines as a problem, big or small."

We are here on earth for a reason or reasons. A purpose according to my perception is not one particular thing you were called to do. It can be a multitude of tasks that have to be completed. One way or another we all have an impact on the way that we view life as a whole. What I want people to realize is that if you don't start doing things on purpose, you'll never know what it is that you're trying to do.

We must fail to understand what winning is. We must win to feel what it is to fail. If we don't ever win, we won't be able to identify when we are. You have already developed a mindset that you are never going to win. Therefore how do you identify when you are a winner.

When you're a winner and you don't fail, you are used to winning. Your interpretation of failure may feel greater than someone who has always failed. So when the individual who failed constantly begins to win, It may not seem like it's a huge deal to the individual who is used to winning. The beauty in failing is that you can win also.

The ugly thing about failing is that it tears down your confidence. When you fail over and over and over again, you almost feel like giving up, but you must fall in order to learn how to get up. My whole life I always felt like a failure. I never could do anything right. My mother played a role in that because she was a single mom and she wanted me to get it. So I was forced at a young age to mature faster than other kids my age. I didn't understand why she was so hard on me until I had a daughter of my own.

It was hard for me to grasp the idea of what a "kid" was. I constantly felt lonely and unloved. I never could understand, but always knew that I was missing something. What I didn't know is that I was also carrying my mother's wounds and emptiness. I am sure that she felt like she was also on survival mode because she was a mother and a young woman trying to raise a younger woman.

What we fail to realize is that as a society, we have inherited the generational pain. It is something that happens inevitably. Although we brush it off, it affects us as whole. Systematically, we have become accustomed and have found alternative ways to cope with internal burdens that we have mentally, physically and emotionally have taken on.

Now that I have an understanding of the pain that my mom carried from the trials and tribulations she faced, made me realize that it made her durable. I try my best to explain to my daughter how not to fail opposed to identifying when she failed, because our kids will fail. However, they will continue to fail if they aren't given the instructions or tools to do otherwise.

I fell into the trap of feeling like a failure. Everything I did didn't seem like it was enough. My mother didn't have the instructions, but tried her best to apply what she did know. It wasn't enough for me! At the age of twelve I told my mother I wanted to commit suicide one night after we got into a verbal conflict. She told me that I am crazy and that she was going to take me to see a psychiatrist. In that moment I felt like I was crazy and didn't belong. What saved me is that I didn't know how to commit suicide, but in that moment I felt that if I were dead, then things would be better.

I didn't feel like I existed. I was extremely frustrated with myself because I truly felt like a bother. My mother never took me to see a psychiatrist. I can say that I am happy that she didn't because it could have been for the worst. I will never know, but it is something I thought about.

Failure made me angry, bitter and very insecure. I thought all of the worse things about myself. I thought I was ugly. I hated my hair. I didn't have the nicest clothes like everyone else. I didn't have both parents in the home. I didn't like the skin I was in. People did say nice things. My mom spoiled me and tried her best. As I matured, I began to look at my situation differently.

It wasn't until I was twenty six years old, when I told my mother for the first time that I was raped at the age of fifteen. In that moment I was brought back to the time. I remember like it was yesterday, when he picked me up and said that we would hang out. It was more than that. I went into his house. Suddenly he said that I was acting differently. When I entered the room, it was dark, cluttered with junk and clothes from what all I could see.

I could also hear people in the back rooms. I didn't understand where I had gone wrong. He began to kiss on me and I tried to stay calm because I was afraid. The TV was loud and I was lying on my back. He became more aggressive and looked into my eyes. I knew by the way that he looked at me that something was going to happen. I expressed to him that I was a virgin and that I did not want to have sex with him. He told me to shut up and put a ring on my finger that he took off of his.

I began to cry as he pulled out his manly parts, raw and inserted it into my womanly parts. When I tried to yell he covered my mouth. I began to cry hysterically as I tried to fight him off of me. He then slapped me in the face and continued to stroke. I cried and he stroked until he was finished. I cried myself asleep because he refused to let me leave. When I woke up that morning I was happy to be alive. The room was still dark and filled with a mess. When the morning passed, I stayed in that dark place for ten years.

When I experienced my first anxiety attack, I began fighting for my life back. I remembered that I was on the phone. My mother began to cry and expressed that she had been raped too. Once she explained that to me, I started to understand why she treated me the way she did because she also felt like she failed. My mother wanted to protect me.

"In reality, we all have particular things that lies within us, whether it's pain, guilt, happiness, burdens, regrets,etc. What we do with it is up to us as an individual."

We shouldn't blame anyone for the things that happens to us. However, there are situations where you could feel betrayed or like someone has taken advantage of you. We have to take the obstacles and fight through them and try to understand why we had to go through them instead of wondering why it happened. If we can't make sense of situations that we have faced at that moment, it's okay. It is imperative to know when to move on and let go. The key is that you have to acknowledge what has happened. Learn how to forgive.

Life is a puzzle and the more that you try to force them together, they bend and fold. Then the outcome makes no sense. We have to take our time to self-reflect. Our failures, pain and weaknesses are important to think about. Mental health, anxiety and failure are a few examples. It is a part of life. It is how you manage your thoughts, environment, time and relationships with others.

I would be lying if I said I don't experience these things. I have read titles of books such as how to beat anxiety once and for all or depression, or how to become rich in 30 days. Granted I have read some of the motivational books briefly and they have helped me to an extent. However, I am human and I will continue to face barriers, obstacles, failures, etc. It doesn't just go away!

For a long time I thought I could kill the anxiety and depression once and for all. It later led me to feeling more anxious and depressed. The purpose of this book is to share my stories with you and to explain that at the end of it all you're not alone, but you must keep pushing yourself forth.

You will have days where you experience feelings of anxiety or depression. Don't let your thoughts control you. Get control over the life that is destined for you. Be in control of your thoughts by meditating on positive ones. The forever comes when you make the conscious decision to choose to be alive.

Life has its ups and downs. We are not given a crystal ball, but how would you ever know if you could have won if you gave up. Life is beautiful and I thank God for keeping me. I want this book to touch your heart as well as other people's hearts. I want the world to understand that we live in a society where there are many individuals from various backgrounds and journeys that are suffering due to the stigmas that they carry.

No matter what your situation is, whether you were abused, incarcerated, raped, abandoned, financial unstable, homeless, drug abuser, etc; whatever has caused you to give up, whatever caused you pain to your mental

"I believe that God has the final say so. I am not God and I am not here to make promises. I am here for reason of voice, motivation and empowerment."

health; I want you to know that I love you and to not give up. If no one believes, you I do.

Ashamed

"Do What Matters"

I am ashamed at my life. I am in my twenties and I don't have a house, a nice car or am I making less than 25k a year and I'm struggling. That is the truth. I will not hide who I am. I never did and never will. I want you to know that it is okay to be ashamed. Sometimes I look back at my life and I cry, laugh, smile and frown. I have had many mixed emotions about my life.

I wanted to always understand why are there birds? Why is there land? Why do people work? The "whys" are important. Don't be ashamed at not being born perfect because it does not exist.

Why be ashamed and drown in pain and worry? I could answer for you. I don't want you to answer the questions right away. I want to open your mind so that you can think about it. I am ashamed that when I was younger at the age of five, my grandmother was a drug addict, my grandfather was a drug dealer and I had to stay at his house when my mother worked. I'm ashamed because someone threw a brick and it could have killed me.

That's how I know that God is real. I am ashamed that I grew up in lower class poverty. I am ashamed that I didn't have a father growing up because the man who claimed to be my father was absent from my life. It wasn't until I got older that I met a man who I knew in my heart was my father, who took on the role.

I am ashamed that I wasn't taught how to love or be a woman. I am ashamed that my mother wasn't taught how to live or be a woman. I am ashamed that I was an alcoholic, raped and sexually frivolous. I am ashamed that a man has abused me at the age of 21. I am ashamed that I didn't have the finer things in life and got made fun of.

I am ashamed that I had children at the age of fifteen and my second at twenty-two. I am ashamed that I couldn't give my kids the life that they deserved. I am ashamed for being depressed and suicidal. I am ashamed that God gave me chances, but I could not see them because I was numb. I am also ashamed that none of my relationships have worked out.

I am ashamed that I was an emotional wreck and violent towards others.

I am ashamed that I was verbally abusive. I am ashamed that I had to seek therapy to figure out that I was suffering from PTSD. I am ashamed that my closest friend committed suicide in 2016, following my brother's death in 2017 and my elementary school sweet heart in 2017.

I am ashamed that I have gone through so much. I am ashamed of not having a life that seems normal. I am ashamed of my life. I am ashamed that I am ashamed of the life that was given to me.

Imagine being ashamed of all of those things from the age of five to your adult years. It is deadly in itself. I am ashamed to say that I became vulnerable because of the daily anxiety attacks I had. I am ashamed to say that I began taking a med for depression because my depression alone was killing me. I was at a point in my life where living didn't matter to me. I already felt dead in the inside. I hated my life and I didn't care about living anymore. I wanted to commit suicide.

After my brother died, I really began to question my life. I began to go back to church and I was blessed to find one. It was helping me. Then life happened and I was in a horrible relationship, arguing constantly, increased anxiety attacks and became pregnant which led to abortion. I was tired and just felt hopeless. I stopped focusing on my dreams and I partied more. Once that relationship ended I became angry. I had inappropriate and sexual interactions. I didn't care!

I had a reality check. I took the hurt and pain that I was experiencing and took it out at the gym. I began to get in shape and was feeling confident and happy. I began dating someone from my past but didn't feel like it was the right time for me. I eventually went back to school and I wanted to get the fun out of my system. There is no such thing?

You have to make that conscious decision and have a disciplined mind. Until the week I felt my life flash before yes. In the process, I began to have stomach pains and aches. I couldn't sleep because I was self-destructing.

That week I felt that it was ending for me. I went out with a friend from church. I got extremely drunk and was doing about 75 mph on a ramp towards my house. I crashed the side of my car and my tire popped. My friend was behind me luckily and he was able to bring me home. In that moment, I was ashamed of my life and did not know where I was heading. I had not been sexually active at that time.

I self-reflected and repented to God for all of my wrongdoings. A few days later something came over me almost like God laid his hand over my whole body. That day I decided to make a conscious decision to be celibate from sex and alcohol. I felt ashamed that it took me that long to wake up.

> *"After being ashamed of so many things for so long, I decided that the only thing that I should be ashamed of, is being ashamed that I was ashamed of things that are a part of life. "*

Compelling Allure

Facing Self

"Embrace Your Ugly"

Look at yourself in the mirror and understand that you are who you are. Accept it! Facing yourself is one of the hardest tasks to execute. We can't blame anyone for the things that we have gone through. Whether you have been raped, abused or been through any kind of obstacle, facing it could be difficult. This is life and we aren't born to be perfect, but to get through the many challenges that we will go through. It is imperative to reflect. We often avoid reflecting on the person that we are, where we came from and also where we are

189

heading. If you allow yourself to get caught up in that life you'll find yourself wishing that you had reflected.

Don't wait until the last minute because time is valuable. We never know when our time is up. There is so much that you can learn from looking deep within yourself and admitting to yourself that you have flaws. Acceptance is key. Feelings come and go.

Some days you may feel like you aren't where you want to be. Some days you may feel that you have everything you need. When you accept things for what they are, you develop a new perception. The lens that we often look through is scratched, blurry and gives us a false images. Perception is deception! Remember that!

Just how you look at things can deceive

you from your true reality. We then end up living our lives wishing that we could make changes. I want you to take time and begin to value yourself. Understand that you are unique in your own way. If you could accept one thing about yourself, whether it's a characteristic, talent, or hobby; whatever it is, embrace it with love. Why? Because it's a part of you.

You have to be willing to accept yourself. It is necessary. Facing self is the most vulnerable position that you can ever put yourself in. I use surrendering to God as an example. Please realize that we are in a world of sin (flesh). Therefore under the spiritual Realm (God), life is looked at differently. In reality the world exists differently. Not everyone is spiritual and not everyone believes in Christianity. Also not everyone is religious.

Whatever your position is it is important to be 100% with yourself no matter what your stance is. To face yourself, it is about breaking down the layers from the external to the internal. I did this by looking at myself in the mirror, looking outside of myself and not allowing my thoughts to create a bias or a stigma that I had created for myself based on self-victimization through my experiences.

When you are able to look at yourself from the outside as if you're looking at someone else, you start to notice things that you never noticed before. Sometimes it could completely turn you off and cause you to feel some anxiety or even become depressed. In this moment, stop and take a deep breath because sometimes we don't realize that there are particular issues that we don't tackle right away.

I would like to say it's never too late but I would be lying. Sometimes it may be late, but you have an opportunity when you act on it in positive, healthy ways. Some people don't have the opportunity to face themselves.

So if you're reading this book, you have a chance, so seize it! It is an automatic to look at yourself in the mirror. What you see is what you think and what you think is what you see. How I felt inside was horrible and I always felt sad, depressed, lonely, betrayed, unworthy, hopeless, insecure, destroyed, oppressed, suicidal, etc. You get the point.

When I looked at myself, it was impossible for me to see the beauty within myself because I was allowing my mind to dictate my reality. When facing self, you have to literally come out of your comfort zone. Admitting the ugly scenes about you from a spiritual, social, and physical aspect as well as your actions could be distasteful. I had a really good friend from college tell me that they had stopped believing in religion because they could not live up to God's standards. This is a very sensitive topic to touch on so please prepare yourself and open your mind for just a few moments.

I have always been hard on myself. Although I wasn't brought up in a Christian home and I didn't go to church every Sunday. I went to church occasionally with friends or family members, but one thing about me is that I always tried to prove myself whether it was to my mother, or on a spiritual level, or friends and family members. Often times I felt like I was not living up to what others expected of me. Perhaps if I just focused on what expectations I had for myself. If I would have created those boundaries in the mindset early on I could have avoided a lot of heartache.

There's always would of, should of and could of; but what about now of. Live in the now of where you are in your life at this moment. We live in a world where we want to fit the median of life. We want people to accept us.

"Wouldn't it be nice to be liked by everyone?"

Remember you have to accept you.

Unfortunately we do not live in a perfect world nor are we perfect. So when I thought about what my friend from college said to me, it made me wonder. I believe that if we cannot live up to someone's standards, should we completely eliminate our self? How can we disqualify ourselves? What gives us the authority? Is it a choice led by faith or fear?

I think often in times in life we give up on our greatest visions with fear. If we cannot complete every single task in an orderly fashion or like someone else we may feel that we cannot execute the plan. Don't live a comparative life. Your life will look different from the person you're next to. There is nowhere in the Bible that states that we have to be perfect. However, God wants us to walk in His footsteps to be more like him. We can't be God, so therefore all you can do is try your best to be you and put God first before anything.

There is sin in this world so therefore we are going to sin until the day we die. When facing yourself, are there things that are small or are those things big? I am not saying that is okay to sin, but it is a natural part of life. You want to be able to face yourself. For example, I have the tendency of throwing things on the ground. I know it's not right, but sometimes I do it anyway.

Am I sinning? Can I live with myself after? Yes! Do I sometimes feel guilty about it? Yes. What are your flaws? What things do you need to change? Who do you need to remove out of your life in order to clear your path from overconsumption? Face your truth and be you!

When becoming successful it is impossible to not get any cuts or bruises along the way. What is success to you? How do we define success? Is success sustainable? Is it physical or is it mental? Self-deprivation will suppress our dreams and hopes. We feel like we can't do something perfectly or become in denial of our reality. The point that I am trying to make is that in life we just have to go through the process.

The key is to believe in yourself so when you are in the mirror looking at yourself, you're facing yourself. What you will see is not your permanent and final destination. Don't allow your circumstances which are right in front of you to dictate where you are going and your future. It doesn't work that way.

If God was that simple, He would reveal everything to us all at once. How would we be able to sustain the information and the wisdom that He gives us? We have to go through the experiences in order for Him to teach us. Therefore when you're facing yourself, you have to understand that some days you're going to look ugly. You're going to feel ugly, but that is temporary.

The one thing that I love most about life is that you have the power to change your mindset if you work hard enough for it. Who you were an hour ago does not mean that you cannot change the person you are going to be a minute later. Sometimes we have to fight harder than others.

Here's an important key, don't live a comparative life as I mentioned previously. Live up to your own measures and means. Not everyone is destined to be like someone else.

We are all unique in our own way. Look at yourself, accept you for you and clean up the garbage in your mind. Get rid of the junk. Don't allow your garbage to overflow.

Sometimes you have to be willing to throw it away. Don't become a hoarder, a person who can't get rid of unnecessary things.

When you are willing to let go of some of the baggage, you create space. Don't fill it back up with more garbage because you then become a trashcan. Replace the bad with the good. If you don't, this could lead to depression, anxiety, overthinking, self-deprivation, suicide, ugliness, hurt, pain, trauma, and unnecessary situations.

Look at yourself in the mirror, face yourself and whatever it is that is hurting inside, you have the power and the choice to say, *"I am done."* It is not easy work. I repeat it is not easy work. It's going to be hard. It's going to be a process. It's not going to take 30 days. It may not take a year or two years.

You have to be willing to work and if you are spiritual or religious, you have to be willing to work with God. Meet God halfway. Take care of yourself, love yourself, and face yourself for who you are, accept who you are because who you are is beyond what you see. If you believe in yourself, you can achieve almost any and everything. Have faith as small as a mustard seed.

In life it is so easy to get caught up with the external things in life. You can become something that you are not. You can develop habits that don't align with the person who you truly want to be or with the things that you value. It becomes a conflict because you are living a different image, but feel differently inside. You begin to question the person you truly are. It took me quite a while to accept that

I was trying to be someone that I wasn't.

Sometimes in life people fall in love with the

person they think that you should be. They

don't necessarily fall in love with the person

that they truly are or even the person that they

strive to be.

"In the process of facing self, ask yourself, "What do I value?"

Fighting Back

"Confront Your Inner Battles"

Why are you giving up? As soon as something goes wrong, everyone is afraid to keep moving forward. I cannot name one success story in my life that was not a fight. Not one. My life was never easy. Not because I didn't have a choice, but because I put myself in situations that was a total fight to get out.

It is so easy to create a situation where you constantly put yourself in a deeper hole. We will inevitably put the blame on others because it easy. For example: *"If I had my father in my life at a younger age I wouldn't*

203

had go through all of this heartache." True!

However, God allowed me to go through it. If I didn't experience the situations that I did, I don't know if I would have been ready for the world. So instead of feeling sorry for myself, my alternative was to fight back. In reality I had no other choice. Please be willing to admit your wrong doings by not putting the blame on others.

Naturally there are things shifting, things that are happening underneath the surface. This could be pain, regret, fear and obstacles. Things are constantly shifting even when we least expect them to. Although I experienced great pain while working on myself, the pain, regret, fear and obstacles began to shift.

Compelling Allure

I became aware, conscious and wanted to find the good in it all instead of focusing on the bad. Often times we look at the end results of people's lives and we automatically assume that they were given everything or were handed a silver spoon. It is impossible to see the hurt from the outside because some people have mastered putting on the costume.

It is the things that are underneath the surface because they're not right in front of us. If they were right in front of us we would never seek to find out the truth.

If you think about people who don't have the opportunity to fight back due to being unaware simply because people may assume that they are okay. Later on you end up finding out that they had also been suffering. We then are in total shock.

We get caught up on the exterior. We are all struggling as a society. It is important to understand that fighting back is not easy. I became tired of living the life that other people wanted me to live. Getting very drunk, the sexual relationships I had, the very disgusting words that came out of my mouth, the people I may have hurt; I was the one who was truly losing.

The people who cared saw the problem. When they attempted to help, I continued with the behavior. If you notice that you are hurting others through your actions, why continue? The people who were broken inside along with me were unable to see that there was a problem because they suffered just as I did. Is there any justification for that?

I am sure that if you are reading this

book you could probably relate. I had to fight for my life. I wanted to live. I became tired of losing. If you want a life for yourself you have to be willing to fight. The fight isn't easy. You'll look back and see who's fighting with you, only to find out that you're fighting alone.

The inner battle is something that you have to address and you will need some support from positive influences such as friends, family, therapist, etc.

When fighting back it could make you feel weak in the process. It is the most vulnerable feeling that a person could endure. I had to repent and turn to God to uplift me. I knew that I needed a life jacket. Even though I knew there was a possibility of drowning, I still took chances that I began to drown in. If you had a choice, would you drown purposely?

I wanted more and needed more. I didn't realize that I would remove the people who I thought supported me out of my life. They were part of the attack. I was afraid to confront my inner battles. They enjoyed winning the battle. I told myself that, **"Girl you know how to thump."** Why are you acting like a punk! In order for me to achieve my Bachelor's degree, I had to fight as a single mother with two kids, fathers who were absent and low income.

The first step was I had to remove the negative distractions out of my life. The main distraction in my life was alcohol. Alcohol was my best friend. When I felt mad, it hyped me up. When I felt vulnerable, I was able to have sexual relationships without feelings attached (so I thought). When you have sexual relationships from a spiritual aspect, it is a soul tie. When angry, alcohol supported me.

The second step I had to turn my back against the crowd and had to focus on my family (my two beautiful kids). They drove me to make the changes. I then had to become sober and focused. This was not easy but I managed to do it. I became laser focused and didn't allow anyone to come in the way. Through the process I was still experiencing many battles. I was going through withdrawals, depression and anxiety. It was truly rough and fighting was a struggle. There were plenty of times I wanted to give up.

Although I was making changes in my life, my judgment was defective. I had to go through the emotions and had to stay strong. When I applied to college and became focused, people started to literally drop out of my life. It became very lonely. Without my own understanding, my life began to shift. I had a few friends in my circle that tried their best to be supportive.

However we began to hang out less and talk less. I couldn't understand why they weren't fighting with me or as hard as me. What I learned that there are inner battles that are deeper than the exterior battles (bills, finances, support etc.) I realized that I had to thump on my own. When enemies who were against me jumped me (sex, alcohol, negative relationships). I had to fight and sometimes make peace.

It was difficult because at one point they weren't. I continued to entertain the enemies. I became stagnant and I was comfortable. Over time I laughed because I realized that I didn't want to grasp what was happening in my life. I wasn't holding myself accountable. I was in hell and it was all I knew. So I'm sure you're asking why would someone be that dumb to purposely accept being in a toxic lifestyle.

My answer for destroying myself is because I was lazy, complacent and negligent to my mental health. I also didn't want to fight and I was allowing life to live me. Even though I knew how to fight, I got tired of fighting alone. It had to take something as traumatic as my brother dying for me to fight. I fought and when my brother was alive, he told me to stop stressing and to not worry about him.

"Sis, you got to stop stressing, that stuff will kill you.' Brian J. White. I knew I had to stay strong."

My last year in college, I had to fight when my brother died. I literally was fighting, crawling on my knees, crying and asking to have the strength to keep moving forward. I couldn't sleep. I would wake up in panic screaming. I ended up in the hospital several times because I was stressing and experienced a series of anxiety attacks.

I thought to myself, he said to stop stressing. I remember the day we last spoke over the phone. I expressed to him that I was stressed because I was worried about him. I didn't want him to go back to jail or get killed. My brother reminded me that he would be okay.

In the beginning, it was a struggle. I

couldn't differentiate the night from the day because I ended up in a dark place. Just when I thought the battle was over.

What is it, who is it, why is that you're fighting? I had to fight for my kids because I wanted something so much greater than what I had experienced. As I'm writing this book, I am still fighting. It is my job to make sure that I give as much information that I can give to help someone out there struggling with the things that I have went through, still going through and will go through.

Fighting doesn't end, but the battles become easier. It's not what you went through, what you're going through, but getting through the challenges even when you don't know what the outcome will be. I would be a bold face liar if I told you that I am perfect and that in 30 days you will be cured.

On a spiritual level, I must prepare you. My belief is that there is only one person who has that power; which is my Lord and Savior. I want you to fight. I want you to fight so hard for what you believe in. Believe in yourself. Know that you have someone out there who supports you. I believe in you!

You picked up this book for a reason. It is not a mistake. I know this is in almost every book and motivational speeches. Seriously this wasn't a mistake. Writing this book wasn't a mistake. Fighting back is necessary. It is always easier said than done. It wasn't easy for me at all as you can imagine.

It is harder, especially when you have experience with anxiety and depression, PTSD, etc. The stigmas alone can literally alter your thought process and literally destroy the person that you are. You can't allow it. This includes the anger, resentment, decision-making, impulsiveness and much more. I had to fight a lot and to be honest I'm not a fighter, but I can fight if I need to depending on the importance for things such as my life. If you're not a person who is a fighter in a physical way, it does not mean that you're not fighting.

In order to fight you have to have a goal in mind you have to ask yourself, what is it that you're fighting for and then you have to choose your battles wisely. The only way that you can choose your battles wisely is by going through them and seeing which ones benefit you.

For example there are certain relationships that I had been in that I fought for that I thought was not worth fighting for.

However, I do believe that we face many situations. We face them all for a reason, but it does not mean that you want to continue to go through the same battles each and every day.

I love the saying, " *Choose your battles wisely.*" I can attest to that. Some of my battles felt like I didn't have a choice. I had to reflect on whether or not I was benefiting from my battles in positive ways.

Sometimes we have to go through things in life to know what not to do. The battle that we have control over is the one that is in our

"Fighting can be very exhausting to the mind, body and spirit. If you are going to fight for something, fight for something that is worth fighting for."

mind. Fighting back within the mind means positive influences and energy, meditating,

216

working out and eating healthier are some examples that helped me.

Although you may go through obstacles and face traumatic situations in life, you have the power to fight the battles within the mind. So you have to differentiate which battles you need to go through in order to get to the next level in life.

Compelling Allure

Harmony

"*Humble Yourself and Listen*"

What is true Harmony? Harmony was a place that I never knew I would understand. If you knew better, then you would do better so they say. It took me a long time to grasp the idea. How could you understand something that you've never seen or ever experienced? But instead of me living a life that I thought was for me, I lived a life for what I thought people thought it should be.

I began to live up to other's expectations. Later on in life that led to nothing but self-destruction!

Harmony is the place that I look at in the future. Harmony is something that everyone should have the opportunity to experience. It is something that should be everlasting in your life. I would not have been able to experience the true essence of Harmony if I had not gone through the many obstacles that I have gone through.

We go through many challenges in life. I personally do not regret them because If God had not allowed me to go through particular situations; I would not understand the beauty of life.

The life I am able to embrace is now filled with the things I choose through the wisdom of God. Don't get me wrong, I am not perfect in the eyes of a person. However, I no longer have to be a victim of living for others' satisfaction or entertainment. I have had the privilege of Harmony, because I've been at rock bottom.

I've been stripped naked. I have had things taken away from me. I've been so down that I lost who I was as an individual. I got sucked up into a life that I thought I should be in because of what others thought about me.

Harmony is about being true to you. Harmony is about doing the things that make you happy in life. It meant not making others happy according to what they want you to do in your life. They are accountable for their own life, which you should be accountable for yours. Be accountable for your actions so that when you move forward in life you can understand the true happiness of what you should receive in life. Harmony!

When you have Harmony in your life, you're able to appreciate the beautiful things in life. Everything that I saw that I had lost in my life was not actually a loss, but it was a process that I had to go through an order to reach that point in life where I was trying to get peace. What I can say to you right now is that don't ever underestimate where you are going. True Harmony for me was accepting my reality and knowing that there were things that I could change. I did not have to be stuck in a place of pain. It's also about realizing that being true to yourself is important.

Showing gratitude for the things that exist in your life, it's about living in the now and not defining your happiness based on things you think you should have at this time. Instant gratification does not guarantee happiness.

How do we sustain a life of happiness? It is to constantly work towards it. Having an outlook on what you would like for taste, look, smell and feel like. I hope that this book will lead you to a life of peace, acceptance and understanding in hopes to increase your faith.

I want you to understand that we are all human and that we all in society experience different journeys. We come faced with different challenges, but that should not identify who you are as an individual. If there was one place that I can choose to be it would be in a place where I feel one with myself. I would want to feel a sense of acceptance from the inside out. This book allowed me to do that because I was able to reflect and pull out the greatness in myself.

Often times when people seek harmony

they tend to look in the wrong places. There are materialistic things that can truly mask true harmony within. People do this by spending money on temporary pleasures. I can agree that for a moment external things can be reassuring because it's instant. Unfortunately, materialistic things don't last forever because if it did, we would seek peace within. It is hard to come in contact with yourself. We get filled with things that are not positive for us. I used alcohol and hanging out with people who did not share the same interest as me.

I came to a point in my life when alcohol became an annoyance, burden and enemy. I had to let go. Know when to let go. I also brought things to fill those empty places. It was nice in the moment to have particular things, but over time it became draining. Once those places became empty again I was seeking more. Maybe a new car, a pair of new shoes, different hairdo; only to find out I was left without anything.

Only a physical form of myself because my soul was tormented. Imagine for a moment of someone stripping you naked for everything that you have! How would you deal with that? Do you think that you would be able to recover from that? I am here to tell you no! It's not a good feeling to have important things taken away from us. One thing we can recover from is emptiness within. You can begin to gain the inner peace.

It isn't always simple, but I will tell you there is a way. I then received a message from God. It was right after I almost lost my life. I was drinking and partying hard, hanging with people who also enjoyed doing that. They aren't the ones to blame for the story I am about to share with you. Hence these are the people who filled my emptiness on two dollar Tuesdays, thirsty Thursdays, Fridays and Saturdays. I felt complete to have a social life because I felt that I was a part of something. I didn't know what harmony was.

It wasn't until I was alone and realized how empty I really was. It wasn't until I became sober again. It is when I realized that I had been filled with toxins and was literally drunk on life. I was *"living my best life."* The truth is I was living my worst nightmare. The last time that I almost came in contact with death is when I drank during an early evening at a happy hour until around midnight. At this moment, I no longer had the capacity to hold on. I was in a total hole. If you're wondering how this experience led me to harmony I will reveal shortly.

At this point I was in fact dead. I lost my inner self and I became an enemy to myself. I was slowly killing myself purposely. It was like an autoimmune attack. I allowed my emotions and carelessness to put me in a place of destruction. My pain, hurt and downfalls began to attack my mind. It is common that people get to a very low point. Then there are people who are "perfect". They make no mistakes. Their life is filled with abundance. They are happy and whole! This is

"Love, peace, harmony and stay humble."

what we see on the outside. *"We don't know what a person goes through internally."*

After I faced this situation that I was battling with, I prayed to God. Now I'm not saying this is the only way for everyone, but for me it changed my life. I promised to give my life to the Lord and to do right by him. I began to focus more on myself and I made sure that I was intentional. Being intentional can change your life, if you focus on the thing that truly matters. It is not easy! None of it will ever be easy.

You will encounter bumps and bruises. You will fall, fail and get off track. You have to get back on track, because we all make mistakes. You should seize every moment and cherish it.

The key is to strive not to continue to make the same mistakes and strive to be the best version of yourself. We also should encourage one another. You have the ability to overcome the things that may bring you down externally and internally. Seeking harmony is hard work and it is something that has to be worked on, each and every day. It is easy to fall in the trap of doing the right things and then stop. I have done it on many occasions.

I found harmony by facing those flaws, my imperfections, carelessness and abuse. We can't forget our past, but we can accept it. We also can't forget the pain that we have encountered. We also deserve a chance at life. If you want to succeed in life, if you want to feel good within, it is necessary to do the work. If you don't do the work, unfortunately you may suffer.

However, I believe that if you choose not to put in the work for your life, that's a choice. Some people are okay with it. I am not here to judge your decisions. I am here for reason. If you want the maximum out of life it's going to take maximum dedication. It's a fact! You will continue to look for things that give you temporary pleasure. Remember that it doesn't last forever. Harmony is about accepting the things that take place in our life and staying strong to get past obstacles.

I hope that this book finds you well. I also pray that whatever it is that you have faced in your life that you use it as strength and to not allow it to identify who you are or dictate who you are going to be. I can't stress enough that it takes a lot of hard work. It's about changing your mindset. When thinking of the pain that we have gone through, or the battles that we faced in midst of negative thoughts, or even mental health problems; it isn't an easy pill to swallow.

We have to find that place that is within that allows us to be filled. Seek love, compassion and understanding. Begin to love yourself, do the things that matter and fight for peace. Don't settle for the external things in life because you will never endure true happiness based on my personal experience. Whatever it is that you want in life for yourself, you can do it! Pain and Harmony feeds off of each other, except being stuck in pain doesn't fill your inner self. Pain is the fuel to success.

Compelling Allure

Love Your Trauma

I hope that this book finds you well because you deserve it. When you experience any level of depression or anxiety, it can feel like bondage. Don't allow yourself to be stuck in a world of worry or fear. Life will hit you in a way that truly hurts if you allow it. Had I not gone through the trauma that I had been through; I would have never known what it was.

The opposite of trauma is healing, which means that if you never experienced pain, if you haven't been through anything, therefore you won't need healing. It's not until you go through life experiences that you really get to feel pain.

What is trauma? I think that based on my experiences, it is something that feels painful and unforgettable. Pain feels like a third degree burn depending how deep your pain is. I think that trauma feels like a deep cut which is a different kind of pain. Both are wounds and they heal over time; some quicker and some slower.

When I think of trauma, I think of a different experience. How do we heal internally? How do we heal externally? We treat it and hope for it to heal. It is important to have faith in the process because God knows the beginning and the end.

Therefore nourish your pain; don't allow it to get infected with negative things. A cut is the same process. We have cuts above the surface and beneath the surface. Both require a healing process. Everything is a process, but there will be beauty in the end. We have to take care of the things we go through and use it as strength.

If you allow the pain to grow, the pain gets worse and makes it difficult for you to turn back. Know when to let go and when to move on. Losing three of my loved ones destroyed me. In memory of Brian Jeremy White, 02/06/2017, has made me passionate about the spiritual journey that I am on. Embrace the journeys that you come to face with. Every journey is unique and you could be a blessing in someone else's life.

"If My People, who are called by My Name, shall humble themselves, and pray, and seek My Face and Turn from their ways; Then I will hear from heaven, and will forgive their sin and heal their land."
II Chronicles 7:14

ACKNOWLEDGEMENTS

I am thankful and give all of the glory to God for making this book possible. I am grateful to have such wonderful people in my life; who has actively supported me through this wonderful, spiritual, and joyous journey. Most importantly my Kids, Kianna and Noah inspired me.

My parents, friends, family and professional influences had a positive influential impact, also my sister Kahrisma and my brother Brian (RIP).

Everyone who collectively believed in me made this possible. Thank you, and God Bless!

―――――――――――――――

"Trust in The Lord with all thine heart, and lean not unto thine heart and lean not unto thine understanding."
Proverbs 3:5"

―――――――――――――――

Made in the USA
Lexington, KY
08 December 2019